REMARKABLE
VILLAGE
CRICKET
GROUNDS

Author's Acknowledgements

My grateful thanks go to my partner, Jill Haas, who read all the articles and made very many helpful comments which improved them considerably. My contacts represented a wide cross-section of the community. These very different individuals were united by their love for cricket and the conviction that their ground was the most beautiful in the country. My sincere thanks go to (alphabetically by club):

Simon Pengelly (Abbotsbury C.C.)
Rob Dunn and John Philpin (Abinger Hammer C.C.)
Philip Chandler (Aldborough C.C.)
Peter Higham (Alderley Edge C.C.)
Paul Wileman (Ambleside C.C.)
Martin Binks (Arthington C.C.)
Bill Starr (Audley End C.C.)
Bill Brooke and Geoff O'Connell (Bamburgh Castle C.C.)
Robin Cross (Bearsted C.C.)
Andrew Dann, Rory Kerr, Vic Heppenstall and David Mitchell (Belvoir Castle C.C.)
Guy Mawhinney (Benenden C.C.)
Barry Leaning (Bilsington C.C.)
David Hughes (Blenheim Park C.C.)
Mike Barnett (Booth C.C.)
Doug Sherring (Bridgetown C.C.)
Tony Greaves (Bude North Cornwall C.C.)
Jeremy Daggett, Sam Stockdale and Ed Williams (Burnsall & Hartlington C.C.)
Ian Cook, Jo Kevan and Chris Millns (Castleton C.C.)
Bryce Rundle (Chagford C.C.)
Richard Cooke (Cholmondeley Castle C.C.)
Mike Beard (Clumber Park C.C.)
Martin Gladwin (Cockington Pk C.C.)
Nigel Dixon (Coniston C.C.)
Richard Hoyle (Copley C.C.)
Ryland Wallace and Lawrence Watts (Crickhowell C.C.)
Jonathan Hill (Doo'cot C.C.)
Vernon Powell (Dumbleton C.C.)
David Whittington (Ebernoe C.C.)
Brian Woodford and Robin Eaton (Elmley Castle C.C.)
John Suckling (Firle C.C.)
Chris Bidwell (Fulking C.C.)
Richard Geffen (Goodwood C.C.)
Peter McAndrew (Great Budworth C.C.)
Jim Trinham (Hagley Hall C.C.)
Kath Gower (Haworth C.C.)
Richard Williams and Robin Corrigan (Holkham Hall C.C.)
Rob Moore (Honley C.C.)
Sir William Worsley and Stuart Prest (Hovingham C.C.)

Chris Deverell (Ickwell C.C.)
Keith Richardson (Keswick C.C.)
Dave Doughty and Dave Cook (Kildale C.C.)
John Ross (Kinross-shire C.C.)
Roger Sykes (Leigh C.C.)
Elsie Smith and Mark Melly (Linkenholt C.C.)
John Ashton (Luddendenfoot C.C.)
Malcolm Caird (Lurgashall C.C.)
Raymond Bartlett (Lustleigh C.C.)
Andy Tuck (Lyndhurst & Ashurst C.C.)
Robin May and Alex Spice (Lynton & Lynmouth C.C.)
Anthony Morris (Marchwiel & Wrexham C.C.)
Keith Hughes (Menai Bridge C.C.)
Tony Wade (Meopham C.C.)
Peter Glass (Midhurst C.C.)
Alan Barmby; Karl Afteni of Mountnessing Mill (Mountnessing C.C.)
Jon Russell and Nigel Robinson (Mytholmroyd C.C.)
Michael Butler (Nettlebed C.C.)
Tony Richards (North Devon C.C.)
Ewan Green (North Nibley C.C.)
Phil Evans (Northop C.C.)
Chris Hagues (Old Town C.C.)
Simon Wardley (Oxted and Limpsfield C.C.)
Richard Kelso and Betty Jackson (Patterdale C.C.)
George Hammond and Jake Cheesman (Penshurst Park C.C.)
Steve Caygill and Paul Hedley (Raby Castle C.C.)
Vinny Hanson (Rawtenstall C.C.)
Simon Hicks (Saltaire C.C.)
Phil Evans and Robin Willacy (Sedgwick C.C.)
Darren Chapman (Sennocke C.C.)
Mark Wilkie (Sessay C.C.)
Elisabeth Skinner and Ollie Bruce (Sheepscombe C.C.)
Zai Ali and Jean Tennant (Sicklinghall C.C.)
Anthony Griffiths (Sidmouth C.C.)
Tim Clarey (Snettisham C.C.)
Peter Riley (Southborough C.C.)
Martin Darlow (Southill Park C.C.)
Harry Mead and Charles Allenby (Spout House C.C.)
Craig Sprigmore (St. Philips North C.C.)
Tony Revell (Stanway C.C.)
Nigel Martyn (Tilford C.C.)
Tony Webb (Ullenwood Bharat C.C.)
Jon Slater and John Carlisle (Upper Wharfedale C.C.)
Chris Ward (Warborough & Shillingford C.C.)
Alastair Gibson (Warkworth Castle C.C.)
Mark Fishwick and Martin Cuerden (White Coppice C.C.)

With special thanks to Jill Rooney of the l'Anson League and Mike Amos of the *Northern Echo*.

First published in the United Kingdom in 2018 by
Pavilion
43 Great Ormond Street
London
WC1N 3HZ

ISBN 978-1-911595-56-4

A CIP catalogue record for this book is available from the British Library.

10 9 8 7 6 5 4 3 2 1

Reproduction by Rival UK

Printed and bound by 1010 Printing International Ltd, China

This book can be ordered direct from the publisher at www.pavilionbooks.com

REMARKABLE
VILLAGE
CRICKET
GROUNDS
— BRIAN LEVISON —

PHOTOGRAPHS
DAVID MAJOR & JILL MEAD

EDITOR
FRANK HOPKINSON

PAVILION

Contents

Introduction

Cricket, like no other sport, is woven into the landscape of this country. It is resolutely embedded in the villages and rural outposts, hewn into the upland hillsides and planted firmly on the lawns of great country estates. A quintessential rural English village has a church, a pub, a village shop, a red phone box and cricket played on the village green. These days it might be a struggle to find a village post office as well, but despite the relentless squeeze on time, village cricket teams are fighting a stubborn rearguard action.

Remarkable Village Cricket Grounds is the companion title to *Remarkable Cricket Grounds* (2016) and is a compendium of some of the most breathtaking and singular village cricket grounds in England, Scotland and Wales. In truth we could substitute the word 'idyllic' for remarkable as unlike the previous title we haven't gone to the extremes of the UK to find the most southerly, northerly, highest or lowest cricket grounds. Coldharbour in Surrey, close by Leith Hill Tower, is proud to be the highest ground in the south of England at around a thousand feet, but there are no emergency reserves of oxygen held behind the club bar, and it is included for its sylvan setting and views, rather than its distance above sea level.

LEFT: Coldharbour C.C.'s opening batsman Peter Snook launches another one deep into the bracken on Leith Hill.

ABOVE RIGHT: Bearsted C.C. give fair warning to cars parking alongside The Green during a match.

RIGHT: Arthington in Yorkshire has a typical 'old school' wooden pavilion, however teas lady Eileen Barraclough does have running water.

When it comes to biggest and smallest, the villages that compete in the Lancashire League will surely have the largest spectator capacity and we visited both Ramsbottom and Rawtenstall as part of our cricketing odyssey. When it comes to the smallest ground, again it is hard to say without visiting them all; it is much easier to compare pavilions. The tiny pavilion at Baldon Green in Oxfordshire (see page 222) might qualify as the smallest cricket pavilion, though the marvellous green, complete with thatched cottages and welcoming Seven Stars pub, is rarely used for cricket these days.

The same could not be said of Arthington in Yorkshire which has one of the classic, small wooden pavilions, where there is running water, but only from an outside tap. Smaller still was

the original wooden pavilion at Sicklinghall in Yorkshire which was burned down by vandals in 2016. However while the blow might have been the death knell of a lesser club, Sicklinghall has bounced back with remarkable fortitude and played the 2017 season from two Portakabins that they are slowly growing to love.

The Ship Inn at Elie in Fyfe will always be the wettest cricket ground, as the team plays on sand in the harbour when the tide is out. It is the only village cricket ground where a stray crustacean or seaweed might be found embedded in the corridor of uncertainty. Ironically, when photographer David Major stopped by in the summer of 2017 rain had stopped play in the annual match between Elie and Earlsferry. Taking pity on the poor Sassenach who had trooped north in a pilgrimage to see one of the idiosyncratic stars of *Remarkable Cricket Grounds*, the lads duly agreed to take the field… or strictly speaking, beach, for some photos.

The Ship Inn take their cricket very seriously. Elie and Earlsferry are neighbouring villages on the Firth of Forth and there is specific demarcation of which house can play for which village. And they are certainly the only pub-based beach team with an electronic scoreboard. The Poplars cricket team in Wingfield, Wiltshire, is a pub team whose fixture list is not determined by the tide tables. Many pub teams ramble from ground to ground, playing other pub teams on a rented square. The Poplars has its own compact cricket pitch attached to the pub which the team has been playing on for the last 51 seasons.

However 51 years is a blink of the eye compared to some of the clubs visited in the book. Some of the grounds included have remarkable histories. Cricket at Goodwood in West Sussex dates back to 1702, while the game was played at nearby Firle in 1725 or earlier. A letter survives from the Duke of Richmond – owner of the Goodwood estate and one of early cricket's most important

patrons – to his friend Sir William Gage, owner of the Firle estate, challenging him to a game. In his acceptance letter, Sir William mentioned that he was 'in great affliction' having lost a game the previous day. He lost the next match as well. Undeterred the Gage family still own the Firle estate, and the official cricket club dates to 1758.

Those who dip in and out of this book in a random fashion will be rewarded with a tremendous variety of grounds from lush parkland to wind-blasted heath. Those taking it in alphabetical order may notice coincidences thrown up by Murphy's Law. There are only two windmills in the book, at Mountnessing in Essex and Meopham in Kent. Murphy's law has ordained that by arranging the book in an A-Z fashion, they are featured on successive pages.

TOP: The unique harbourside scoreboard at The Ship Inn, Elie.

ABOVE: The pitch is prepared for the annual Elie versus Earlsferry cricket match, one of the few grounds in the country where a fielder might come across a boat at deep midwicket.

Similarly the two Lancashire League clubs with beautifully preserved relics of 19th-century industry nearby, Ramsbottom and Rawtenstall, are conjoined, as are two clubs with almost identical elegant manor houses on the boundary, Nettlebed in Oxfordshire and North Nibley in Gloucestershire. Thankfully the great Palladian palaces of Holkham Hall (Norfolk) and Hovingham (Yorkshire) have Honley's unique pagoda in between them.

Although many of the grounds have glorious bucolic scenery and classic architectural backdrops we have included one remarkable ground in Cheshire where the mighty structures of modern industry tower over the cricket pitch. At Winnington Park the ground is overlooked by the old ICI plant, now Tata Chemicals, and it is striking to see cricket, which is associated with wide green spaces and 200-year-old cedars, being played seemingly in the middle of a chemical works.

In many respects this volume is like a Domesday Book of village cricket. Former TMS contributor Pat Murphy wrote the excellent *Rothmans Book of Village Cricket* in 1992 and quite a few of those clubs are represented within these pages.

The most noticeable change from 1992 to 2018 is that twenty-six years ago there is not a helmet or a forearm guard to be seen in any of the photos and tea was taken with teams sitting together on benches in the pavilion. These days, the essential tea ladies may not have changed, but teas seem to be a more buffet-style, alfresco affair. Another essential reference in our research, Jonathan Rice's *Pavilion Book of Pavilions*, makes it quite apparent that village cricket has moved on, and the standard and

ABOVE: The view looking towards The Cricketers pub at Meopham in Kent.

facilities of many clubs' pavilions are far above what they were in the past.

Alas, there are some clubs in both books that are no more, whose former grounds are waiting in hope for a chance revival. Goodnestone in Kent played their games in front of the elegant 1704 Goodnestone Park house and its distinctive topiary, but ran out of players. A similar fate has befallen Hurstbourne Priors, west of Andover in Hampshire. If ever there was a ground that justified the much-used 'quintessential' epithet then it is Hurstbourne Priors with its gated entrance, thatched pavilion and the parish church of St. Andrew peeping over the trees. Apart from the lack of players in rural areas, the village has suffered from its location less than two miles away from Longparish C.C., a team that

BELOW: Holkham Hall in Norfolk is a Palladian beauty with an elegant, award-winning new pavilion.

has twice visited Lord's for the village knockout final.

To the north, in the Cotswolds, there are two grounds in even closer proximity that would be worthy of inclusion in any national tourist board advertising campaign. Stanton and Stanway are only a mile and a half apart, and while Stanton offers views of the Jacobean Stanton Court and the distant Bredon Hill, Stanway's cricket pitch lies in the fiefdom of Stanway House with its classic Jacobean Stanway Gate. The cricket club is a little way down the road and has a pavilion donated by J. M. Barrie after he took a hat-trick at the club, a feat that is rumoured to have involved a certain connivance from the locals to achieve. A summer afternoon sat watching an innings at each club could not be better spent.

In compiling this book we hope to have included the most photogenic village grounds from around the country. Three of our choices are backed by William Wordsworth, Laurie Lee and J. M. Barrie, so we feel on firm ground for those. But we will undoubtedly have missed out some gems along the way. Settle C.C. in North Yorkshire, starting point for the epic Settle-to-Carlisle railway line, is perhaps one that slipped through the net. So for whatever reason if we have omitted your own particular favourite ground, which has moved a visiting poet laureate to tears, or was championed by the late John Arlott or E. W. Swanton, please let us know. At some time in the near future there may be a second innings and author Brian Levison, like a cricketing version of the Trident missile system, is in a state of constant readiness; his deckchair is packed.

Frank Hopkinson, 2018

TOP: The vacant ground at Hurstbourne Priors in Hampshire, photographed in August 2017.

ABOVE: The cricket ground at Goodnestone as viewed from the elegant garden of Goodnestone Park, before its demise.

ABOVE LEFT: Author J. M. Barrie donated the pavilion at Stanway C.C. in the Cotswolds.

Abbotsbury

Dorset

Back in 2004, the *Wisden Cricketer* chose Abbotsbury as Britain's Loveliest Cricket Ground. Much praise went to the club secretary and groundsman, Mike Lydford, whose daily shift kept the ground in immaculate shape. All these years later he is still producing an attractive venue, overlooked by St. Catherine's Chapel on the hill above. The chapel is thought to date to the late 14th century and was built as a retreat by the Benedictine monks of Abbotsbury Abbey.

The area, just a shingle's fling from Chesil Beach, was used as the setting for the 2015 film of Thomas Hardy's novel *Far from the Madding Crowd*, starring Carey Mulligan and Matthias Schoenaerts, and is part of the Ilchester Estate belonging to Charlotte Townshend. Mrs. Townshend is the only person in Britain, other than the Monarch, entitled to own swans because the only managed colony of mute swans – Abbotsbury Swannery – lies within the estate. It also explains the choice of a swan as the club's logo. The estate charges only a peppercorn rent and the heir, Simon Morrison, is the Club President. Contact between the estate

and the club is very amiable and includes an annual match.

Abbotsbury draws its players from nearby Bridport, Weymouth and Dorchester and a couple of the local villages. It runs just the one senior side which plays in the Dorset Cricket Board League on Saturdays and midweek T20 cricket in the Dorchester Evening League. The club was formed in the 1860s and has played at the Westfield ground since the War. The pavilion used to be a chalet on a nearby farm till it was transferred lock, stock and barrel, to its present site, since when it has been substantially refurbished.

Club captain Simon Pengelly, who has played for the team for 20 years, sums up by saying: "You couldn't ask for more - a good bunch of blokes playing in beautiful surroundings."

Club: Abbotsbury C.C.

Abinger Hammer

Surrey

Abinger C.C.'s ground on the A25 near Guildford typifies all the timeless qualities associated with traditional English village cricket. Situated in an area of Outstanding Natural Beauty, the ground is ringed with trees and the River Tillingbourne meanders along the bottom of the ground to form a natural boundary.

This perfect setting emerged only after much hard work, according to an excellent club history by Mike Woods and Geoff Dunn. The club was formed in 1870 and played in Abinger Hall until 1959, when it was forced out by a dispute. It was not till 1962 that it found a new home on the village green, augmented by an acre or so of an adjoining field. Funds were raised locally and a grant received from the National Playing Fields Association to pay for the construction cost. Frugally, the old 1952 pavilion at Abinger Hall was taken down and moved to the south-western corner of the new ground.

Work was completed in time for the 1964 season, but in the interim the club had to play most of its games away, causing a fall-off in local membership. By the 1970s, the club, which runs

three sides over the weekend and a midweek T20 team, was again on an upward path. Recent successes include three VCL (Village Cricket League) championships. In 1977 the club concluded that upgrading the existing pavilion would be impracticable. Ever perfectionists, rather than compromise on standards, it chose to build a new clubhouse in a better position, which was opened in 1978 with a celebrity game featuring Rohan Kanhai among others.

The ground, which is also used as the village green, is maintained on a completely voluntary basis by club members. Equipment includes a new Baroness outfield mower, purchased for £10,000. An interesting organisational problem arises whenever Ride London uses the A25 for one of its large-scale charity cycling challenges. With something like 25,000 amateur cyclists taking part, security along the route is strict and access to the ground is closed off, even for the cricket team. So if there's a home game that Sunday, the whole side camps out on the ground overnight. Happily, the club receives a reasonable grant for the inconvenience, which makes it all worthwhile.

If pressed for a highlight, the club fondly remembers the visit of the full New Zealand Test side in 1983, which brought three thousand spectators and great names like Sir Richard Hadlee and Martin Crowe to the ground.

Club: Abinger C.C.

Aldborough

Norfolk

Not far from Cromer on the north coast of Norfolk is the village of Aldborough whose cricket club proudly traces its existence back to 1797 or maybe earlier. A game involving local players was recorded in *The Norfolk Chronicle* of 1792, although the club's masthead claims no more than, 'Prior to 1797'.

Cricket has continued on the village green ever since. The club currently runs a Saturday XI in Division 4 of the Norfolk Cricket League, where it holds its own in mid-table, and a Sunday XI, consisting mainly of more mature players. Another XI enjoys a midweek 20/20 bash. The club also has a well-developed junior section for boys and girls. All this represents an encouraging recovery from 1992 when *Rothman's Book of Village Cricket* reported that the village ran two teams and cricket interest was on the decline.

A visitor glancing around the ground will search in vain for a pavilion. This gap is filled thanks to a creative relationship between the club and the local Black Boys pub, which lets Aldborough use specially converted outhouses for changing rooms and equipment storage. In return the club holds meetings and post-game wind-downs in the pub to everyone's mutual benefit. In the close season, president, Billy Hammond houses the club's rollers, sightscreens and other heavy duty items in his barn. Further support comes from the parish council which owns the ground and lets the club play rent-free.

The playing area is bordered by cottages, some of which are within six-hitting distance. The occasional broken window has led to an unusual ground rule for friendlies and T20 games. By all means have a slog. Clearing the boundary will earn you six – but it's six and out.

Club: Aldborough C.C.

RIGHT: A Then and Now comparison from the 1950s as local boys stage their own game.

Alderley Edge

Cheshire

In the Cheshire countryside, not far south of Manchester, is a group of towns and villages sometimes known as The Golden Triangle. George Osborne, the former Chancellor of the Exchequer, was once the local MP, appropriately enough as the Tatton constituency is reckoned to be the most affluent area in the country outside the Home Counties. Alderley Edge, in particular, has a high profile, with local property much in demand by Premier League footballers, actors and multi-millionaires.

Although United and City are inevitably the main focus of local sporting attention, the village is home to a highly successful sports club based at Moss Lane. Founded in 1870 as a cricket club, Alderley Edge freely admits 'it was set up by wealthy mill-owning Victorians for the toffs'. Locals wishing to see their masters at play were forbidden to advance nearer than a particular oak tree close to the boundary. All this changed after World War II and now the club boasts over 1300 members who use its extensive facilities for tennis, hockey and squash, as well as cricket.

The 7.5-acre ground was originally leased from the De Trafford Estate at a peppercorn rent, but Alderley Edge managed to buy the freehold for the modest sum of £3,500 in 1960. The playing fields are surrounded on all sides by residential housing, largely screened by a rich variety of trees. The location is made especially memorable by the presence of the Edge, a dramatic, wide red sandstone escarpment to the south. Tucked away over the entrance is the original compact half-timbered scorers' box which provides an excellent view over the ground, providing you can elbow the scorer out of the way and squeeze into it. The striking clubhouse, with bell tower, dates from the Victorian period.

The club has three senior sides and topped the Cheshire County League in 1975 – the League's inaugural season – and has won the title on three more occasions, most recently in 2016. With nine youth sides, the thriving youth programme has produced many trophy-winning teams.

The playing area is undeniably county-standard and is used by Cheshire CCC. In 2017, Freddie Flintoff, who lives locally and is a club member, brought an All-Stars team including Michael Vaughan and Steve Harmison to the ground for a 20/20 game to raise funds for Prostate Cancer UK.

Club: Alderley Edge C.C.

TOP: The striking clubhouse, with bell tower, dates from the Victorian period.

Ambleside

Cumbria

Ambleside, in the heart of the Lake District, is Wordsworth country, where the poet lived and worked for decades. Sheltered in the ridge of the Fairfield Horseshoe and overlooked by Loughrigg Fell and Wansfell, the Rydal Park playing area is one of the most beautiful in the country. The ground is part of the Rydal Estate owned by the LeFleming family, who were Wordsworth's landlords when he lived at Rydal Mount, and are committed to supporting cricket.

Formed in 1858, the club has probably been playing at Rydal Park since the 1900s. Club secretary Paul Wileman says the area's surpassing beauty isn't all good news for the club. "The town is such a popular tourist and holiday home area that locals have been priced out. We do our best to attract new members, including taking a Freshers Week stall at the Ambleside campus of the University of Cumbria." On a more upbeat note, the teams the club plays today in the Westmorland Cricket League (WCL) are the same ones in the 1949 fixture list.

Following an unbeaten season in 2017, Ambleside was promoted to Division 1 of the WCL after a nail-biting victory over Netherfield. The club has won the Division 1 title on two occasions, the first time in 1949 when Ambleside all-rounder and local legend Arnold Burrows led the side. Another stalwart is 74-year-old Paul Allonby, the current groundsman, who has been associated with the club since he was 14. "Paul spends all of his summers – and winters – maintaining the ground in its excellent condition," says Wileman. "He's also something of a local hero, helping to rescue a teammate, Ron Treptow, from certain death when he became trapped in a canoe in the icy waters of Great Langdale Beck."

The modern-looking pavilion was built and self-funded by club members in the late 1960s. The club has also received welcome funding from Sport England towards the cost of a new roller and drainage improvements, and from the Kelsick Educational Foundation. The ground is transformed on the last Thursday in July when the annual Ambleside Sports Foundation Festival takes place. There's fell racing, hound trailing, wrestling to local rules and all the fun of the fair. No cricket – but the club runs the bar and gets a significant boost to funds.

Club: Ambleside C.C.

Arthington

Yorkshire

The cricket ground at Arthington opened on June 9th 1864, the same day as St. Peter's Church on the other side of Arthington Lane. St. Peter's was declared redundant by the Church of England in 2005, and later became a Coptic church, but Yorkshire's other religion appears to be thriving in Arthington. The club plays in the Theakston Nidderdale League and both its senior sides were recently promoted. It also runs a Wednesday evening team, which plays T20 in the Harrogate and District Evening League.

Located near the River Wharfe, the ground is part of the Arthington Estate, whose Grade II-listed hall was built around 1795 by John Carr, architect of the impressive Harewood House only a few miles away.

Before World War I, members of the Sheepshanks family, previous owners of the estate, lived in a hall close to the ground. They eventually fell out of sympathy with the number of occasions a well-hit straight drive landed on their lawn and insisted the club realign the pitches from north-south to east-west. Given that many club cricketers' stroke of choice is a slog across the line, the decision was questionable and the ball continues to land in the front garden

on a regular basis. In September, the setting sun can be so dazzling from one end that the captains often agree that bowling takes place from the other end only.

The current owner of the estate, Roger Quarmby, is club president and very hands on. He has personally mended the pavilion roof and built new toilets. A current plan aims to replace the pavilion – an assembly of 120-year-old wooden huts – with a new structure, including separate changing facilities for girls. A replacement for the ancient Ransome mower is also on the club's wish list, as is increasing the current nine pitches to ten or eleven.

They love their cricket in these parts and when the rest of the cricketing world quietly packs away its kit for another year towards the middle of September, Arthington is just beginning its Cricket Festival, four or five weekends of friendlies extending the season into mid-October. The Festival, set up in 1989, was the brainchild of the club's secretary for almost 30 years, Martin Binks MBE (conductor of the Leeds Symphony Orchestra for even longer). Now in his seventies, he still plays for the Second XI, as does Dennis Nash, who manages a nagging length at medium pace at the age of 80. His wife Elizabeth and Eileen Barraclough are the club's much-valued tea ladies. A long-time participant in the Festival was Doghouse C.C., so-called because the secretary took on the position knowing 'it would put him in the doghouse'. Doghouse's last-ever game was against Arthington in 2016. Arthington, however, continues to go from strength to strength.

Club: Arthington C.C.

FAR LEFT: Arthington's much-valued tea lady Eileen Barraclough gets on with the most important element of any cricketing afternoon.

FAR RIGHT: When you are too young to appreciate the qualities of a cover drive, you can always turn a kitbag into a bean bag and watch videos on a phone. Four-year-old Matilda might be interested to know that cricket bags can be a lot bigger and more luxurious than that one.

BOTTOM: A canvas sightscreen inside the boundary in Arthington C.C.'s picturesque ground near Pool-in-Wharfedale.

Audley End

Essex

Audley End House was originally Walden Abbey, a Benedictine monastery which had its roots in Norman times. After expansion and refurbishment in the 17th century, it was palatial enough for Charles II to rent when he attended the Newmarket races. Today it is a third of the size it was then, but, even so, remains a handsome building which contains many interesting period exhibits on public display, including cricket memorabilia such as Georgian bats and old-style wickets with only two stumps.

Cricket began here in 1842 when Charles Neville, a keen cricket-lover and subsequently 5th Lord Braybrooke, laid out a pitch in front of the mansion. The very next year the MCC visited and played regularly against the estate side throughout the 1840s.

When he became Lord Braybrooke, Neville revealed one or two idiosyncrasies in the way he managed the cricket. Since it was his ball, so to speak, he arbitrarily determined when matches started and finished and when tea was taken: he may even have ruled on lbw decisions from the boundary. After his death in 1902, cricket continued, but faced a change in 1948 when English Heritage bought the property from the 9th Lord Braybrooke. However, the club's right to play on the ground rent-free was carefully

protected, though with one major change. The river Granta runs through the middle of the park and in 1979 the club relocated from the house side, where it had traditionally played, to the far bank, at English Heritage's request.

The estate team lasted until 1948, and the club now draws its players from local villages. It runs just the one senior side which plays in the Cambridgeshire League, winning as many as it loses. For a long time the club also played in the League's winter 6-a-side tournament, winning 17 titles in a 20-year period and even getting to the Lord's final, where it came close but lost. A youth side was discontinued some years ago, but the good news is that there are plans to revive it shortly, also that a new pavilion is planned with funds raised locally.

Touring sides from all over the world are keen to experience cricket in this graceful setting designed, by among others, Capability Brown. The cricket ground has many visitors, undoubtedly enticed by the mouthwatering homemade teas provided by the team of four ladies, led by Gemma Hill.

Club: Audley End C.C.

Bamburgh Castle

Northumberland

With a village population of only about 300, Bamburgh Castle C.C. is hard-pushed to raise a team to play in a Saturday league. In fact, a decade or so back, shortage of players forced it to pause cricketing activities for the first time since it was founded in 1860.

Fortunately, there were some crafty minds behind the scenes. The club now runs one side and has made Sunday its match day with occasional midweek games, offering the chance of non-league Sunday cricket to anyone who might fancy playing in the mighty shadow of the castle. 'What nicer way to spend a summer Sunday afternoon?' as the club's home page says.

According to the secretary Geoff O'Connell, keen young players under 20 have rushed to join the club, making up about half the side and contributing significantly to the team's success – it won over 90 per cent of its games in 2017. But given the ubiquity of the young, that can sometimes be a weakness as well as a strength. Not long ago, one of the most promising youngsters scored a double century, only to leave soon after because he'd been recruited to play, not for a rival team, but the band Mumford and Sons.

The magnificent castle, which spreads across 9 acres and is in constant demand as a location for period films, has had an extremely long innings dating back to Anglo-Saxon times. Owned by the Crown for centuries, it was sold to the Forster family in 1610, and passed into the hands of the engineer and inventor, Lord Armstrong, towards the end of the 19th century. While landscaping of the Green was in progress, his horse died and was buried on the edge of the square, which is now known as Dobbin's Corner.

Ties with the Armstrong family are very close and the current owner of the castle, Francis Watson-Armstrong, is the club president. In return for being allowed to play rent-free, the club mows the whole green twice a week on behalf of the croquet, bowls and other activities which take place there. A brand new ride-on John Deere mower was purchased for £25,000 in 2015 for that purpose, a huge sum for such a small organisation. Without a lease on the green, Sport England funding wasn't available, but the money was raised within a year through a combination of activities and local donations. Fund-raising matches on Bank Holidays continue to supplement the club's income and come complete with sumptuous cream teas catered by Susan Parmley, a baker, and wife of the club scorer. The club has no more than four or five away games each season as it is inundated by requests from Australian, Indian and American teams to play in such an imposing venue.

Club: Bamburgh Castle C.C.

LEFT: Playing cricket on Bamburgh Green is like playing a favourite sport in an episode of *Game of Thrones*.

Bearsted

Kent

Bearsted is proud to be one of the oldest active cricket clubs in the country. It has always played at this graceful ground surrounded by period houses on all sides, even if the square has been re-orientated once or twice.

The club's official birth date is Monday 14th August 1749 – the day when the Eleven Gentlemen of Bearsted played the Gentlemen of London at the Artillery Ground, Finsbury Square, London, for one guinea per man. Unfortunately, the club, which regarded itself as local champions, overreached itself and London won 'with great ease', according to the *Whitehall Evening Post* report.

For a hundred years or so, the Green was very inconveniently bisected by a footpath. But in the mid-1870s, it happened that four of the team were Parish councillors. In next to no time, an order was passed to grass over the path, though a trace of it can still be seen beside the pavilion.

Many famous names are associated with Bearsted cricket. Alfred Mynn, 'the Lion of Kent', played and lived here for many years till his death in 1861. His outsize figure features on the village sign. A. P. 'Titch' Freeman, the great Kent and England leg-spinner, lived in Bearsted after his retirement in a house called 'Dunbolin' and played for the club occasionally.

Arguably, the most influential of Bearsted's famous residents was Sir Pelham Warner, captain of England in the 1900s. Many professional cricketers came to play on the Green at his invitation, including the 1929 South African touring team. Another less conventional visitor was Baroness Orckzy (1865-1947), author of *The Scarlet Pimpernel* books and an early Women's Rights supporter. She and local suffragettes reportedly invaded the pitch during a game.

The club plays Saturday cricket in the Kent County Village League, running two teams, and

one Sunday side in the Kent Village League. There are several colts teams for boys and girls. The infrastructure clearly encourages young players to progress and in 2017 both skippers for the senior teams were former colts. The square has ten pitches and the spacious and comfortable pavilion dates back to 1958.

An excellent painting of the ground by the well-known cricket artist, Gerry Wright, hangs in the clubhouse. It was commissioned to celebrate 250 years of cricket at Bearsted and appears on the cover of the club's celebratory memoir, *Dedicated to the Continual Enjoyment and Preservation of The Green*.

Club: Bearsted C.C.

RIGHT: One of the fascinating aspects of photographing cricket on Bearsted Green is that it can look like so many different grounds depending from which angle the photograph is taken. Compare this view from behind long-off, looking towards the Holy Cross church and the image below, which is taken just a few yards to the right, from behind long-on, looking towards the oast houses.

Belvoir Castle

Leicestershire

The Normans built the first of the four castles to have occupied this site with its commanding view over the surrounding countryside. The castle is in Leicestershire but not by much; only a few miles away is the Three Shire Oak, where Leicestershire, Lincolnshire and Nottinghamshire meet. Belvoir means 'beautiful view' in French, but the Anglo-Saxons settled for the earthier pronunciation "beaver", which has stuck to the present day. The current castle is a Grade 1-listed building and home to the Dukes of Rutland, who have lived here since the early 16th century.

The cricket club plays in spectacular wooded surroundings with the castle high up in the background like something out of a fairy tale. Notable among the many trees is an imposing sycamore behind the bowler's arm at one end which earns six if hit on the full.

No-one knows exactly when cricket was first played here, but a cricket ball dated 1875 still exists, which was presented to 'F. Adams for Best Bowling'. Like many sides attached to stately homes, the club began as an estate team, Belvoir Estates. The club, which rents the ground from the estate, now runs three senior teams on a Saturday, a Fourth XI for friendlies and one Sunday side. A thriving junior section ranges from the four-year-olds, the Bees, up to the Under-17s, and once included a very young Stuart Broad. With plenty of space, the club is lucky to have two squares, supporting eighteen

pitches between them, plus a third strip for junior games. Having to cater for two simultaneous home games in the ageing 1973 pavilion can put pressure on the tea ladies, but Sally Dann, Sally Neville and other mums, wives and girlfriends handle the stress with aplomb.

The club's cricketing links are more with Nottinghamshire than Leicestershire and over the years many famous names of Nottinghamshire cricket have held benefit matches here, such as Sir Richard Hadlee, Derek Randall, Clive Rice and Eddie Hemmings. The ground is also used for the activities of the Belvoir Cricket and Countryside Trust, under the patronage of the Duchess of Rutland and run by Darren Bicknell, the former Surrey and Nottinghamshire player. The charity organises junior cricket activities for rural communities and the disadvantaged, and cricket practice is often followed by a tour of the castle.

Local club characters include Vic Heppenstall, who gave up playing in the 1960s due to injury and turned to umpiring. He is now 86, has stood in over 2,400 games and still spends his Saturdays in a white coat. His career highlights include standing with Test umpires such as Don Oslear, George Sharp and John Holder, "all of whom taught me a lot," he says.

Club: Belvoir Castle C.C.

Benenden Green

Kent

Benenden in the Weald of Kent is known for its exclusive girls boarding school, but it also has a cricket club that plays on the magnificent Benenden Green. Kent must rival almost any other county with the number of large village greens on which cricket is played, such as Meopham, Bearsted, Leigh, Matfield Green and Southborough to name but a few.

The club's historian believes cricket was played on the green from the 18th century, although the first official mention of an organised club was not until 1798. The greatest claim to cricketing fame came in September 1834, when two players from the Benenden side took on an XI from the Isle of Oxney at their ground just off Romney Marsh in Wittersham.

Richard Mills and Edward Gower Wenman, now firmly installed on the club's badge, played for a £20 purse at 'Double Wicket'. This meant that effectively when one of them was out, that was the end of the Benenden innings. They scored 150 between them until Edward Wenman was bowled for 65. In reply, and with just the two Benenden players on the field, Oxney could only muster 55.

In the second innings it was Richard Mills who was out caught for a meagre 29 as Benenden stuttered to a total of 48. Upwards of two thousand spectators, many placing large wagers on the Benenden men, watched this 'singular contest'. The Isle of Oxney were eventually bowled out for 77 in their second innings, giving

victory to the Benenden men by 66 runs. As a footnote, in 1843 the England team assembled in Benenden to play Kent in a benefit match for Edward Wenman, although this match was played in the grounds of Hemsted Park, now Benenden School.

The club still plays on the traditional village green in front of St. George's parish church and between the Bull Inn and King William IV public houses. Indeed a lusty blow over mid-on has been known to land in the Bull's car park as well as shattering a few roof tiles. The elegant Dutch-influenced Memorial Hall at the other end of the ground acts as the club's pavilion. Built in 1908 it was paid for by public subscription and dedicated to Lord Cranbrook, owner of Hemsted Park.

The club fields a Saturday side (the village side) which plays friendlies, and a (stronger) Sunday XI (the club side) which is a member of the Kent Village Cricket League. There is still a cricket club at Stone-in-Oxney but the two sides no longer play each other, let alone for extravagant purses of £20.

Club: Benenden C.C.

LEFT: The view from St. George's church looking towards the cricket pitch, with Benenden Primary School on the left.

RIGHT: A photo taken from the Bull Inn end of Benenden Green with the Memorial Hall beyond. When not acting as a pavilion, the hall is used for many village functions including bridge club and pilates classes.

Bilsington

Kent

Only Romney Marsh on the south-east coast of Kent lies between Bilsington C.C'.s expansive ground and the English Channel. Dominating the view like an umpire's giant finger signalling out, is a 52-foot-high obelisk, erected in 1835 as a memorial to Sir William Richard Cosway, former secretary to Vice-Admiral Collingwood. Sir William bought the Bilsington Priory estate in 1825, but was killed in a coaching accident nearby in 1835.

The cricket club was founded in 1896 and played at Crump's Ground up to 1939, before moving to its current location after the War. The ground is owned by a local farmer Bill Maylam, who generously lets the club play rent-free. He erected a wire fence to separate the farm from the playing field, which the club uses as a boundary. The fence has to be cleared for a six; even hitting it full pitch earns only four.

Bilsington admits that some of the facilities could do with upgrading. Running water in the pavilion is a relatively recent addition and the nearest accessible loos are in the club's pub of choice, The White Horse, which puts up a team for an annual challenge match. Landlord Gordon Russell is happy with that arrangement, reckoning that each visit sells a pint or two. There's no electricity in the pavilion either and tea is prepared by the players' wives using a gas boiler. "They do a very good job too," says chairman Barry Leaning, who joined the club in 1953 and has been chairman for 20 years. He

RIGHT: The plaque installed at the base of the monument. In 1967 it was struck by lightning, although not during a match.

met his wife Sylvia through the club and she is now Life President.

The club runs Saturday and Sunday sides. The Saturday team plays about 20 games a season in the Kent Village Cricket League of which the club was a founder member. Bilsington has had its moments of glory over the years winning divisional titles, and there have been some good individual performances recently with players reaching 1000 runs in the season. Barry Leaning and members of the team maintain the outfield and the square with its eight strips. One quirk, he points out, is that due to a steep incline, a fielder at the pub end can't see the batsman, let alone the scenic views. But always visible from any part of the ground is the Finger of Doom, the Bilsington obelisk!

Club: Bilsington C.C.

Blenheim Palace

Woodstock, Oxfordshire

A good number of clubs in this book play in the genteel surroundings of a stately home or castle, but only Blenheim C.C. plays in the grounds of a palace. Blenheim Palace is the one building in England not connected with royalty or the church to hold the title of palace (and we are discounting Alexandra Palace). The 2000-acre site was gifted by the nation to John Churchill, 1st Duke of Marlborough and victor of the Battle of Blenheim in 1704.

The various Dukes don't have much of a cricketing history, although the 3rd Duke played 'a great cricket match' on Kew Green against the Prince of Wales in 1737 for a purse of 500 guineas or £100, depending on your source. The Prince won and a newspaper report stated that 'the match was apparently of a minor standard'.

It was the 10th Duke who founded Blenheim C.C. in the 1950s. An estates team had existed before

World War II, but the Duke suggested forming a local team and offered the palace grounds as its home. The players are drawn from Woodstock and nearby villages and regard playing on the South Lawn, close to the burial place of Sir Winston Churchill at Bladon, as a privilege. The club runs just the one team. With no shortage of visiting sides anxious to play at such an historic setting, most of its games are home friendlies against local teams like Steeple Aston and Great

Tew with occasional visits from celebrity sides. The pavilion, admittedly modest with changing rooms but no showers, was built by the club itself and is well-sheltered in a nearby grove. Relations with the estate are very cordial. The club plays rent-free and the palace maintains the outfield and the club the square and the strips.

The club has a nice line in amusing match reports, written by David Hughes, the club secretary. One entertaining read in 2017 claimed a world record for the greatest age difference in opening bowlers, one aged 60 and the other 13. What's more, the pair only gave away eight runs off the first six overs.

With the Palace only about 328 feet (100 metres) away, you might think a few windows have been broken, but not so. The worst cricket-related damage was caused during World War II when Malvern school was billeted at the palace. On their staff was George Chesterton, an Oxford Blue and later a fine cricketer for Worcestershire. He took to practising his catching in the library, inevitably broke a window and found out what it was like to be on the receiving end of a few sharp words from His Grace.

Club: Blenheim Palace C.C.

Booth

Yorkshire

Booth C.C. played at a number of venues before settling at the lovely pastoral setting of Broad Fold Park in 1948. The ground had rather a pronounced slope which the club managed to reduce although not entirely eliminate. But it is part of the charm of the ground, as is the curtain of trees at the bottom of the field and the eight-foot-high stone wall on the far side, which provides a good spectator spot, rain or shine. The club played all its 1947 'home' games away while the construction work was in progress.

Founded in 1893, Booth didn't get off to the best of starts when neighbours Luddendenfoot St Mary's dismissed them for 8 runs in their first match. Beginner's nerves, no doubt, because over the years Booth has been one of the most successful sides in the area. It won the Parish Cup and topped the Halifax Premier Division First XI League table on a good number of occasions, most recently in 2016 and 2017, the club performing the League and Cup double in both years. It has a strong playing base, running two Saturday teams and a Sunday side, as well as four junior teams for boys and girls.

Booth also attracts a very good class of speaker to its annual dinner, says club secretary Mike Barnett, and mentions Geoff Miller, Jeremy Coney, Angus Fraser and Paul Nixon. The pavilion is regularly extended and upgraded and fits unobtrusively into the landscape.

A match which lingers in the club's memory is the Booth versus Booths fundraiser in 1957, when the club played a team of cricketers all with the surname Booth, raising £19 for a worthy cause.

Club: Booth C.C.

Bridgetown

Somerset

When Edward Nesfield moved to Bridgetown in Somerset in the 1920s, he quickly noted the lack of a cricket club. As a former Worcestershire county player, he set out to remedy this gross lack of amenities and started to explore the area for a suitable location. It took him 20 reconnaissances of the valley to make his choice, a beautiful pasture surrounded by grazing sheep, hills and trees near a bend in the River Exe.

Nesfield's choice has been proved right over the decades. The ground has won award after award, including *Wisden*'s Loveliest Cricket Ground Award in 2002 and the *Daily Telegraph* Willow Walks Award for Best Village Ground in 2008.

Bridgetown has yet to repeat its success in winning the West Somerset League in 2014, but has been comfortably positioned in mid-table. It can't bring itself to change or modernise the timbered, thatch-roofed pavilion, which dates back to the club's founding, so the men still use the dunny round the back. However, the ladies noticed a big change in 2018. Up till then, they had to drive to the pub in the village to answer a call of nature. Now they have the unparalleled luxury of access to a Portaloo sited discretely behind a hedge.

Ground maintenance continues to be the responsibility of Doug Sherring, the secretary, and Kenny Cross, the assistant groundsman. The 1956 Allett mower isn't in the best of nick but would cost £20,000 to replace. The ECB can't help because the club doesn't own the ground, Sherring says, but he is grateful to the sheep which take up all the dead grass. The rooks are a problem though, because they tear through the top surface of the field to get at the grubs.

The narrow footbridge across the Exe leading to the ground also needed repairs before the 2018 season. That's the route for the players and, more importantly, Jacky Cross's excellent tea baskets. As Jackie is also Club Treasurer and scorer, she must have her hands full on match days.

Club: Bridgetown C.C.

Bude

Cornwall

Flanked by the Atlantic and coastal rocks to the west, Crooklets cricket ground has one of the most dramatic backdrops for cricket in the country.

Bude North Cornwall C.C. was officially formed in 1870, although the first recorded game took place in 1859, a friendly between the club's own players. The original pavilion, built around then, was only a rudimentary wooden structure. But when a lawn tennis club began to use the venue in 1883, it was replaced by a new stone pavilion costing £150. "The ground was in poor condition and needed to be rolled, levelled and fenced," says Tony Greaves, the club chairman. "The work was carried out by members of the club at the significant personal cost of £80."

Now, thanks to funding from Sport England and the support from the town council, the club has a state-of-the-art structure, opened in 2014 by former England Rugby captain and MasterChef Phil Vickery, who began his playing career in Bude. "We're very lucky," says Tony. "Not only do we have excellent teas, but after matches, it's a great place to enjoy a pint watching the sun set over the Atlantic horizon."

With eleven pitches to manage, Greaves, helped by club players, spends 30 hours a week on the ground. He is pleased with some thrifty equipment purchases made over the years, such as the Toro outfield mower bought from a local golf club for £2,000, a 12-year-old square mower and a wicket mower, bought refurbished six years ago. With a commercial rent payable to the local council and £2,000 annual maintenance costs, finances require careful management.

Income is boosted by the T20 Evening League the club organises. Six teams from local pubs and social sides play each other twice, over ten weeks. The club runs two senior sides in the Cornwall County League and also welcomes many touring sides anxious to play in such a beautiful spot. "It's a lot of hard work, but worth it," says Tony. The club remembers a teenage Shane Warne playing for a Bristol side in the 1980s and, further back, the undergraduate Brian Johnston, whose family frequently holidayed in Bude.

The neighbouring Atlantic doesn't make the weather as difficult as you might think. "Very few games are cancelled," says Tony, "it's often said that if they're not playing at Bude, they're not playing anywhere in the county." He does concede that bowlers can find it a little difficult coping with the wind, and tells of one who bowled 18 wides in an over.

Visiting cricket teams will be pleased to know that they have a better-than-average chance of good weather. According to the Met Office, in 2013 the town was the sunniest place in the UK. The club celebrated its centenary against the England Women's XI in 1970 and is scratching its collective head for something special to mark its 150th anniversary in 2020.

Club: Bude North Cornwall C.C.

Burnsall

North Yorkshire

Daggett's field, where Burnsall and Hartlington play, lies in a tranquil vale of the Yorkshire Dales. It is bordered on one side by the river Wharfe, and on the other by Burnsall Fell, with an old five-arched stone bridge forming a graceful background.

Cricket here tends to be of two types. On Tuesdays, Burnsall C.C. plays 'serious cricket' in whites with independent umpires in the Dales Villages Evening Cricket League. On Wednesdays, it's more relaxed when Burnsall and nearby Hartlington form a team to play 'fun cricket' in the Underdales Cricket League.

The Wednesday rules are idiosyncratic and pragmatic, drawn up to suit the local community, many of whom are farmers first and cricketers some way behind. As getting a team together is difficult enough, why upset anyone if you want them to play again? So a batsman can't be out first ball (Law 12a), and 'No LBWs are allowed' (Law 13b). Because everyone must have a knock, batsmen are retired after scoring 25 (Law 12b). Anyone who wants a game gets one and if a side turns up one or two short, the available players are pooled so that numbers are evened up. The dress code is very relaxed with a 'no whites' rule and comfort more important than image. There is no pavilion, everyone turns up match-ready, and afterwards, "It's just back to the Red Lion," says Sam Stockdale, the club captain.

The Burnsall team was founded post-war and joined forces with Hartlington three or four years ago. They used to share the ground anyway so it made sense. But even the combined village populations amount to only about 150.

To suit the farming timetable, games are midweek evening affairs. High points in the club's history include an appearance by Freddie Trueman when he played for nearby Cracoe, and great speakers such as Craig White and David Bairstow at the club's post-season get-together.

The team plays rent-free on the ground which belongs to local farmer Jeremy Daggett whose relationship with the club is "brilliant", says Stockdale. However, the club does cover the mowing costs and ground preparation, carried out by groundsman Thod Gibson, using a 4-foot-wide 50-year-old hand roller.

Clubs: Burnsall and Hartlington C.C.

BELOW: A cricket ground equally beautiful in summer and winter.

Castleton

North Yorkshire

Castleton is one of the many glorious villages to be found in the North York Moors National Park. Within a six-hit of the river Esk in the heart of the scenic Esk Valley, The Cricket Field is a superb location for enjoying village cricket.

Surrounded on three sides by fields and with a considerable slope, the Cricket Field has a spacious, rural feel. Ian Cook had a 35-year stint as groundsman before retiring five years ago. He was taught by possibly Castleton's most famous old boy, Keith Boyce, groundsman at Headingley for many years and one of the best. Boyce played for Castleton in the 1960s, before becoming a groundsman and taking up groundcare professionally. He regularly came back to the club for annual dinners and talked about Test matches at Headingley, including the famous Botham/Willis game against the Australians in 1981.

No-one has a definitive founding date for Castleton, but a clipping from a *Whitby Gazette* of 1898 suggests it was already well established by then. Until the late 1970s, the ground was owned by the Lord of the Manor, the 11th Viscount Downe. It was then sold to the club and the present stone pavilion built. Castleton plays in the local Eskdale League on Saturdays and the midweek T20 Esk Valley Evening League. An Under-14 junior team plays in the Whitby and District Junior League.

Club: Castleton C.C.

Chagford

Devon

Motorists heading along the A30 on the northern edge of Dartmoor will at some point pass within a few miles of Chagford. A cricket lover will surely want to make the ten-minute detour to visit this charming old stannary or tin-mining town with its idyllic cricket ground.

Bordered by Chagford on one side and the moor on the other, the cricket field blends perfectly into the countryside. Cows graze contentedly behind the fence beyond the boundary; beyond them, on a placid summer's day the moor stretches benignly to the horizon.

Locals say Chagford was formed in about 1895 and played at two other grounds before relocating here almost a hundred years later. It was no easy matter creating the current paradise out of what was effectively the edge of the moor. According to club chairman Bryce Rundle, "It's the only flat bit in the area because we made it that way." A sum of £200,000 was raised from local sources and grants to fund the massive earth-moving works needed to reduce the slope and lay the drainage.

Behind the bucolic exterior lies a hard-working and successful club with two senior sides playing in the Devon League. Among Chagford's cricketing highlights are visits from the Somerset county team; a Soweto XI, organised by the former South African Test cricketer and

administrator, Dr. Ali Bacher; and, in 1995, an old England XI, numbering Jim Parks and Derek Randall among the many famous names.

The club also has a very active junior section, Chagford Youth Cricket, formed in 2012 after many years without youth cricket. The membership exceeds 100 young players between the ages of 5 and 15 drawn from a relatively small catchment area. The club's local schools project provides coaches to run cricket sessions during the summer term.

Club: Chagford C.C.

Cholmondeley Castle

Cheshire

The imposing structure that dominates Cholmondeley Castle cricket ground appears to have been there forever – or at least since the 12th century when the lands came into the possession of the Cholmondeley family. But the castle, it turns out, is actually an early 19th-century replica, the creation of the 1st Marquess, George Cholmondeley, who designed it himself.

Cricket has been played here since 1886, first by estate sides and then by the Cholmondeley village side. There was no changing room for the players until 1924, when Lady Cholmondeley gifted a tent which was erected under an oak tree. Soon afterwards the Marquess donated a thatched-roof structure, built over the nearby mere. In 1975, the club raised funds to build the current sturdy timber pavilion which it has gradually improved and extended over the years, although its predecessor is still used as a tea room on match days.

The club fields two Saturday sides in the Cheshire Cricket League, of which it was a founder member, and a Sunday team which plays nearby villages. Currently there are no junior teams, though there have been in the past. "It's cyclical," says club chairman Richard Cooke, who sees a future for a junior section soon.

The estate has very strong racing associations. Ginger McCain, trainer of three-times Grand National winner Red Rum, moved his stable here in 1990, and the best-selling author and former National Hunt jockey Dick Francis was a playing member in the 1940s and 1950s, "our most famous old boy," says Cooke.

One of the season's highlights is the visit of the Lord's Taverners and large crowds have turned out to see big names such as Gladstone Small, Charlotte Edwards and Alvin Kallicharan. The lake, just the other side of the boundary, is a tempting target. Years ago, a spaniel used to retrieve the odd ball that reached it, but no more. "If they do," says Cooke, "we just let them sink," without making clear whether that's the balls or the dog.

Club: Cholmondeley Castle C.C.

Clanfield

Hampshire

It is a curiosity of cricket that everyone remembers the names of Hambledon, Broadhalfpenny Down and the The Bat and Ball inn at Clanfield when recalling the early days of English cricket, even though the club's heyday lasted barely 40 years.

Prior to 1750, cricket was largely the pastime of the wealthy, who played challenge matches against their peers, usually involving high stakes. Inevitably, players were bribed and undesirables attracted. Eventually the Honourable Artillery Company, the leading ground in London, decided not to play further public matches. Into this gap stepped the Hambledon Club under the leadership of Rev. Charles Powlett, the illegitimate son of the Duke of Bolton. Despite his vocation, he had been known to have a flutter on the outcome of matches and even to bet against his own side.

Together with Richard Nyren, a fine cricketer and landlord of The Bat and Ball inn, he assembled a fearsome array of talent, among them the crafty bowler 'Lumpy' Stevens, thought of as the first great bowler in the game's history. He was so accurate that one of his patrons wagered that he could pitch a ball on a feather one ball in four and won his bet!

With players like Stevens, Nyren himself,

John Small, Thomas Brett and David Harris, the Hambledon club became arguably the strongest side in the country, able to beat Rest of England sides. From that base, Hambledon began formulating the laws to control cricket. The middle stump was introduced, benefiting bowlers like Lumpy whose deliveries sometimes shot through the gap between the leg and off stumps; pitched bowling was sanctioned, even though it was not yet overarm; and bats changed from hockey-stick-shaped to the profile used today, though no dimensions were specified. When a Chertsey player called White came in with a bat as wide as the wicket, the Hambledon players were furious but could do nothing. Very soon afterwards the club set the maximum bat width at 4.25 inches (11 cm), which it still is today. Cricket matches were a spectacle which attracted huge crowds and money; and with money came influence.

It all came to an end in the 1780s. In 1787, the MCC was founded and the first Lord's ground was opened. Cricket's focus quickly returned to London and Hambledon rapidly sank back into the shadows. The Napoleonic wars also drained the club of players. Hambledon limped along with diminishing interest and met for the final time in 1797, when the wistful last minutes recorded, 'No gentlemen were present'.

For 116 years, the ground became agricultural land. Eventually, rights to play on the ground passed into the hands of the Broadhalfpenny Down Association, and now a full season's cricket is played by the Broadhalfpenny Brigands C.C. and other sides including youth teams.

The Bat and Ball inn is still going strong too. It bears a distinct likeness to the 18th-century hostelry where the two teams gathered after the match and proudly boasts, 'Home of English Cricket' on its sign.

BELOW: The monument to Hambledon Cricket Club unveiled in 1908 at the time of a commemorative cricket match between Hambledon and an England XI.

Clumber Park

Nottinghamshire

Clumber, near Worksop in Nottinghamshire, is mentioned in the Domesday Book. Its glories include almost 4,000 acres of woods, as well as heath and farmland, the longest double avenue of lime trees in Europe and many unusual species of birds and cattle.

Cricket at Clumber Park is first mentioned in 1824 in the diary of the 4th Duke of Newcastle, a keen fan. It was only a family game but in due course an estates side was formed, followed by the development of a local team in the 1890s, the forerunner of today's Clumber Park club.

The club plays in the spacious park at the rear of Clumber House and has its own glory in the shape of a unique, rustic, log-clad thatched-roof pavilion with a lookalike scorebox nearby.

Clumber Park is thriving and runs four sides on Saturdays and one on Sundays, plus five junior teams. It recently added a second ground to cope with all the fixtures, which can attract as many as 200 spectators. The club joined Bassetlaw and District Cricket League in 2000 and has worked its way up the divisions, with only one to go before reaching the top league. Prior to that it had only played friendlies, but "social cricket was dying on its feet," says club chairman Mike Beard regretfully, "and rather than have no opponents, we joined the League."

Clumber Park would dearly love to expand and modernise the unique pavilion, built in the 1890s, but that is a matter of negotiation with the National Trust which owns the Estate. "Unfortunately, we have no electrical supply," says Mike Beard, "so it's cold water only and no showers."

Although the park is a site of Special Scientific Interest, the area has been identified as a possible source of shale gas. Permission has been granted for fracking surveys which the estate is attempting to block. Local feeling strongly supports the estate and should things ever come to a head, the cricket club, staunch successors of the yeoman of England, will no doubt be in the vanguard of the defence – bats at the ready.

Club: Clumber Park C.C.

Cockington Court

Devon

Set in hundreds of acres of country park, Cockington Court is a beautiful Grade II-listed 16th-century manor house close to Torbay and the English Riviera. Famous for its wide range of unusual trees, it boasts a Jamaican Fiddlewood – the only specimen in Europe – and an 145-feet-high (44 metres) Sitka Spruce, the tallest tree in the area.

Near the house is a dell bordered by lime trees, where Cockington Corinthians are fortunate enough to play their cricket. Founded in 1933, the club was initially nomadic and didn't settle in Cockington Court till after the War. In those days, the wicket was side-on to the house. Though fast bowlers appreciated the downhill run-up from either end, the wicket keepers complained, so games are now played with the magnificent facade of the house behind the bowler's arm. Former club chairman Martin Gladwin, whose connection with the club goes back to the 1970s, says that fielders chasing a cover drive sometimes ease up as the ball races towards the boundary up the side of the slope, thinking it will easily go for four, then have to step on the accelerator again when they find the ball suddenly slowing up. Many of the wonderful trees are inside the boundary and hitting one will earn 4 or 6, depending on whether the ball drops inside or outside the boundary rope.

In the 1990s, the Corinthians' first pavilion was destroyed in an arson attack. Although the local council, who owned the pavilion, was technically responsible for the rebuilding, local clubs and organisations rallied round. Thanks to their fund-raising activities, a new improved clubhouse was built, re-opened by former Test umpire Dickie Bird, who had played club cricket locally after retiring from first-class cricket.

Cockington Corinthians used to play in the Devon Cricket League, but now restricts itself to Sunday friendlies against local villages, although it is looking forward to its first overseas visitors, an Australian touring side. The club ground-shares with Torquay C.C. Third XI, which plays on Saturdays, providing a welcome source of income. Each August the club also takes a stall in the Cockington Fair, which raises funds for local charities. The Fair takes place in the dell and the club makes sure it keeps the square roped off. Ropes, however, were no deterrent to the bride who once interrupted a game to get a picture of herself and guests in front of the stumps.

Club: Cockington Corinthians C.C.

Coldharbour

Surrey

It may not resemble Italy's Stelvio Pass or the climb to Mont Ventoux in France, but Leith Hill in Surrey has a similar attraction to cyclists. Ever since it became part of the route for the annual Ride London cycle race it has become an area where MAMILs gather (Middle Aged Men In Lycra). The Home Counties are not blessed with challenging ascents and so Surrey's steepest roads are the lodestone which attracts them. Coldharbour Cricket Club's pressing task is to get some of them to dump their bikes and put on cricket whites instead.

Coldharbour play just a large smite away from Leith Hill (1029 feet, 313 metres) and is officially the highest cricket ground in the South of England. It is a compact ground and a six-hitter's dream. In the photograph on page 6, opening batsman Peter Snook is on the way to hitting the first five deliveries of an over for six. Sadly the final delivery was pitched in the blockhole and he could only squeeze it out to the boundary for a single and a paltry 31 off the over. Former player Chris Roux has managed the maximum in the past and it's the perfect venue for such a feat.

The club was originally formed in the 1920s and played on the common in the centre of Coldharbour Village. Incorporating the 18th-century tower into its badge, the club moved to its current position in a clearing on Leith Hill in the 1950s. The ground boasts wonderful views across the Surrey countryside, rare amongst cricket clubs which are normally located in valley bottoms. The club leases the ground from the National Trust who own the land and the nearby Leith Hill Tower. After the pavilion was rebuilt in 2007, the club was granted another 50 years lease by the Trust.

Although the club has ample parking for visitors, there is a great walk starting opposite the Plough Inn, an elegant gastropub in the centre of Coldharbour village that leads up to the cricket pitch and beyond to Leith Hill Tower. The club play a variety of friendlies with teams such as Not

The MCC, London Theatres and Quokkas, along with local rivals (in both the cricketing and idyllic venue sense) Leigh and Abinger.

However, like many teams without a junior section, it is running short of players. In the fixture list there is an entry for July 29th which reads 'no match, dratted cycle race'. Club members need to persuade some of the annual passers-by that a bike ride out to Leith Hill could easily be combined with a cheeky little cricket match, and then an invigorating cycle ride home.

Club: Coldharbour C.C.

BELOW RIGHT: A National Trust information board outside the ground directs walkers on to Leith Hill Tower.

OPPOSITE BOTTOM LEFT: The club undertook a serious undergrowth strimming programme last winter as they were losing up to half an hour looking for the ball.

Coniston

Westmorland

Set in the Lake District National Park and ringed by rugged, dramatic peaks such as the Old Man of Coniston and Yewdale Crag, Coniston C.C. enjoys one of the most magnificent settings of any cricket club in the country.

The club was founded in about 1890 and has had its successes over the years, most recently in 2017 when the second team won the Division 4 Knockout Cup. It runs sides in Divisions 2 and 4 of the Westmorland Cricket League, though no longer a junior team. "Cricket, and even football, is struggling at the youth level in Westmorland; over fifty per cent of residences are holiday homes," says former chairman Nigel Dixon, who wears several sporting hats. He is groundsman, umpire and Second XI organiser for the cricket club, as well as being President of Westmorland's Referees' Society. As if that wasn't enough, after a bit of thought he can even explain the cricket league's points system, though ideally you should have a good maths degree. Your points haul depends on whether you won the toss and batted first and won, or batted second and won, or if it was a draw, but a winning draw. Each result earns a differing number of points. And that's the simple explanation!

The ground is leased from the Coniston Institute and is part of a shared area of sports activities. But the real story of the cricket club in recent years is the frustrating saga of its ageing rickety cricket pavilion, described by consultants as 'decrepit'. Nigel makes daily trips to check the water levels in the buckets he places to catch the leaks. The problem, as always, is money.

None of the usual sources offered funding. "We never even had a visit" exclaims Nigel. But he is cautiously optimistic that there is light at the end of the financial tunnel with the help of local fund-raising activities. "The plans are ready and fingers crossed, we should know very soon." It won't be the two-storey de luxe model with verandah originally planned, which would have earned income as a holiday home in the tourist season, but "frankly", says Nigel, "anything is better than what we've got."

Away from the hassle about the pavilion, the club likes to savour everything about its unique setting, from the grandeur of the surrounding fells to the couple of mallards that return again and again to the ground, the only welcome pair of ducks at Coniston C.C.

Club: Coniston C.C.

OPPOSITE BOTTOM: There is little love for the old pavilion which the club are desperate to replace with some 21st-century facilities.

Copley

Yorkshire

Copley Cricket Club has faced a few short-pitched deliveries in its time, not always on the cricket field. Dodging the fast stuff out in the middle is one thing; fending off the bouncers regularly bowled by the British weather is totally different.

Formed in 1880, Copley found itself a compact playing area in a spectacular setting dominated by the Grade II-listed viaduct over the River Calder on the Leeds-Manchester railway line. It

thrived here, building a strong team which has played in the Halifax Cricket League for most of its history, winning the Division 1 title five times in the last 16 years.

The year 2005 was a turning point because Copley became a Yorkshire Cricket Board (YCB) Focus Club. England's famous Ashes triumph caused the junior membership and number of junior teams to increase dramatically and a new girls section was introduced. The ECB and YCB

liked what they saw and in 2011 awarded the club a £340,000 grant towards the £600,000 cost of building a new state-of-the-art community clubhouse.

Only a few weeks later in June – when it was meant to be summer, even in Yorkshire – the club woke up to find the ground and many parts of the new pavilion under 2 feet of water. The club shook its fist at the heavens and got to work, but no cricket could be played till August.

On Boxing Day 2015, even more disastrous floods occurred. "The whole field and pavilion was 7 feet underwater for several days," says club chairman Richard Hoyle. "The ground floor of the pavilion had to be completely rebuilt and the playing areas also suffered damage. It took 18 months to get through this very difficult period."

Copley enjoys its involvement with the community, such as the Food on the Field gala on Bank Holiday Mondays. But it faces difficulties.

With two 'one-in-a-hundred-years floods' in the last five years, it can no longer obtain flood insurance, and fewer adults are playing cricket than in the past. But the club has strong, experienced leadership and no doubt solutions will emerge.

Club: Copley C.C.

RIGHT: The modern pavilion raised to a level beyond the reach of the nearby river Calder.

Cowdray Park

West Sussex

Few sights provoke more interest than a ruined castle, summoning up romantic images of medieval tournaments and sieges defended.

The truth about the ruins of Cowdray House is more prosaic. Constructed in the 1520s in 16,500 acres of West Sussex countryside, the castle was one of the glories of its era and frequently visited by Henry VIII and Elizabeth I. But it wasn't marauding forces that shattered its defences in 1793. Fire took hold during restoration work with only a few paintings and small pieces of furniture saved. Some blamed the catastrophe on a 16th-century curse to destroy the family 'by fire and by water'. The castle has never been fully restored, but the Grade-I listed ruins are open to the public.

Cowdray Park is probably best known as the home of British polo and the Lawns polo field and the cricket ground are adjacent. Cricket in Midhurst has a long history, going back to 1637 when six young men of the town were fined for playing cricket on the Sabbath. The first recorded match of a Midhurst team took place in 1754 and the current club was formed in 1806. It was a powerful force in local cricket for many years, moving several times before settling at Cowdray Park in 1920.

In 2003, the ground was voted third prettiest in England in a nationwide poll and three years later the club celebrated its bicentenary in style with games against the MCC, Sussex Martlets and a Lashings World XI. Visiting Test stars included Richie Richardson, Aravinda de Silva and Philip DeFreitas. To mark the occasion, Midhurst undertook the mammoth task of compiling the complete statistics of the club from 1820-2007, a 520-page labour of love compiled and produced by club member Ian Nixon, based on research by a long-serving club secretary, the late Harry Wilson.

After playing in the Hampshire County League for many years and having considerably contracted in size, the club joined the l'Anson League in 2014, since when the First XI has managed three successive promotions. "Supported by the Cowdray Park Estate, we are lucky to play in such stunning surroundings," says chairman Peter Glass. "We rely on a small number of dedicated volunteers and the club is progressive and an integral part of the local sports scene."

Club: Midhurst C.C.

Crickhowell

Powys

Founded in 1849, Crickhowell C.C. didn't settle in its current home in the heart of the community for almost a hundred years. The decision to relocate from the outskirts of the town was made at the end of World War II, the new venue being Bank Field, which for many years had been used for cattle and sheep grazing and contained a substantial tump rising towards the castle.

The driving force behind the transformation of this land into a cricket ground was D. V. P. Lewis (later Lord Brecon), a pre-war club stalwart and captain. It was he who promoted the move and supplied the heavy plant (from his quarrying business) for the levelling of the field at his own expense. Just beyond the boundary stands the remains of Crickhowell Castle, an important stronghold on the Welsh borders until the Welsh nationalist leader, Owain Glyndŵr, destroyed it in 1403.

The first match played at the ground was in May 1947. The lyrical report in the *Brecon and Radnor Express* read in part:

> 'Fortunate indeed are the Crickhowell Club to possess so delightful a little ground as their new one opposite the Post Office... It has a pleasant environ with the old castle and some large and shady trees in the background; the "square", expertly laid, looks fast and true, and the outfield short and nicely cut. Such a ground is the reward of generosity, planning and enthusiasm translated into action, and when circumstances permit of the erection of a pavilion, it will be complete.'

A pavilion was constructed by 1951, an attractive traditional wooden structure set in the shadow of the castle walls and this served the club well for some 40 years. Eventually, in the 1990s, it was demolished and was replaced by a purpose-built facility for cricket, bowls and tennis. Harmonious relations between the three clubs are threatened only on Saturday afternoons when cricket balls occasionally fly into bowling green or tennis court.

For many years the owner of the cricket field was Jack Price, who charged only a nominal rent and bequeathed it to the town on his death in 1998. Thus today its official name is 'The Jack Price Memorial Field'. During the 1950s and 1960s the club hosted some of the most prestigious opposition in the region. Thereafter, in the era of league cricket, fortunes have waxed and waned and the club runs only one Saturday side today, competing in the Marches League. Cricketers brought up in Crickhowell include two recent long-serving Glamorgan players, Michael Powell and Mark Wallace.

Club: Crickhowell C.C.

LEFT: Crickhowell lies on the river Usk, in the heart of the Brecon Beacons.

Doo'cot Park

Perth

Cricket at Doo'cot Park in Perth, Scotland, dates back to the 1920s. Since then the ground has been home to a number of clubs, but in 2011 five local teams amalgamated to form a new side, Perth Doo'cot C.C., which looks set for a stable future.

The park was a gift to the city from a local philanthropist, cricket-lover and whiskey magnate, A. K. Bell. An accomplished player himself, Bell was a friend of Sir Donald Bradman and his wife, who in 1934 stayed at Bell's home Kincarrathie House, part of the Doo'cot Park estate.

The ground's charming and stylish features include a large, octagonal Grade II-listed pavilion on two floors, stone-built and lined with larch. Designed in 1924 by a local firm of architects, it resembles a dovecote, doo'cot being the vernacular. 'Any shape as long as it is octagonal' seems to have been Bell's motto as he insisted every house bordering the ground include at least one octagonal window.

Behind the dovecote extends what looks like a row of small, stylish villas, but are actually an extension of the pavilion. The extra space is needed because the park is big enough for two games to take place at the same time, meaning two lots of home and away changing rooms, lockers, showers, tea rooms and kitchen facilities are needed. The structure is popular with children who refer to it as the 'tree house'.

Another Australian cricketer turned up at the ground in the 1990s keen for a game because he was so out of form. The nineteen-year-old was allowed to play and soon recovered his touch, scoring 155 not out in a record opening partnership of 223 with regular club player, Gordon McKinnie. His name was Justin Langer and he went on to break the league's record for most number of runs in a season.

The playing area with twenty-five strips is huge: "I've seen smaller county grounds," says club Treasurer Jonathan Hill. It requires a full-time groundsman, Gary Sly, employed by the estate. The club fields three adult weekend teams, runs several junior teams and works with the Gannochy Trust, formed by A. K. Bell, on youth initiatives.

Club: Perth Doo'cot C.C.

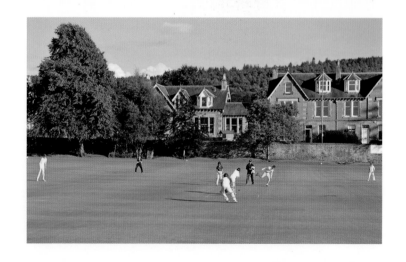

Dumbleton

Gloucestershire

The Dumbleton ground at Dairy Lane is an outstanding example of an English village cricket ground. The playing area is spacious and immaculately tended with a large square of fourteen pitches. Parkland with cedar and lime trees circle the boundary, although a lone oak remains within the playing area, worth six if you hit it full pitch. You can break your stroll round the ground on one of the 24 memorial benches, each dedicated to a past player or club member and each with a flat arm on which to rest your pint.

In a village with no pub, that role is filled on match days by the spacious, sturdy pavilion, which boasts one of the club's prize possessions, an atmospheric water colour of the ground by Jack Russell, the former England wicket-keeper. Behind the pavilion is an unusual water feature; call it a large pond or a small lake. After taking a natural break in the facilities at the rear, John Arlott complimented the club on "one of the best views from any toilet in the country". Unsurprisingly, after a long hot afternoon in the field or a convivial evening, players have been known to jump into the pool to cool off. Beyond that lie the sheep-dotted pastures of Dumbleton Hall, the main hall now a hotel but formerly a stately home.

Dumbleton dates back to 1885 and its centenary was celebrated by visits from Mike Proctor, David Graveney and David Shepherd. In 1934, Wally Hammond held a benefit match here and hit the biggest six ever seen on the ground. Family associations go back generations, always a good sign. At least one member of the Hopkins family has played for Dumbleton from its formation

until the present day. Vernon Powell has been associated with the club as player and chairman for well over 60 years. Dumbleton have recently been promoted to the Glos/Wilts division of the West of England Premier League, which involves driving to away matches across some of the Cotswolds' best scenery. The club has won various trophies throughout the years and is particularly proud of reaching the semi-finals of the 2014 National Village Knockout Cup.

A look at the fixtures diary reveals the club's enormous programme. The club plays 244 games a year, 92 of them at home. It runs three senior XI's on Saturdays, a Sunday XI, a Ladies XI and there are evening and midweek games too. To ease the pressure on Dairy Lane, Dumbleton hires five outgrounds from local villages such as Stanton and Stanway (which both feature later in the book) for £50 a game. There are also 13 junior teams, each with its own coach. Around 140 boys and girls turn up for coaching every Friday evening and make short work of a couple of hundred hot dogs after their workout.

The membership of over 350 and rota of 50 tea ladies provides a very solid infrastructure. The club appreciates all its helpers and one of the season's social highlights is the Ladies' Day Special, when all the tea ladies are treated to smoked salmon and champagne, served by junior members.

Club: Dumbleton C.C.

Ebernoe

West Sussex

A cricket lover with an appetite for food and the unusual should head for the village of Ebernoe in West Sussex on Horn Fair Day. Held on St James's Day – 25th July – each year. The Fair combines the pleasures of watching a hard-fought match between the village team and selected opponents and the ceremonial roasting of a whole sheep. A driver new to the area needs to be alert, though. The road through the village bisects the playing area with mid-on on one side of the road and long-on on the other, so passing cars can hold up play.

Horn Fair Day goes back to the mists of time with occasional hiatuses. With all the fun of the fair for young and old, the event reaches a climax at the end of the 45-over-a-side match when the Lord of the Manor, Lord Egremont, presents the horns of the grilled beast to the highest scoring batsman of the winning side. In the meantime, everyone has been enjoying a post-match barbecue in spades.

Recently, there have been one or two forced changes to these hearty celebrations, according to club secretary David Whittington, who has played in these matches for over 40 years. He admits that, "we've been using plastic horns for the last five years as we haven't been able to find sheep with the traditional horns."

Ebernoe Cricket Club traces its history back to the early 19th century, and when it is not celebrating Horn Fair Day, plays friendlies on Saturdays and Sundays. The club's arch-rivals are Lurgashall, also a village on Lord Egremont's estate, "but they play league cricket and we only play them if they're the opposition on Horn Fair Day," says Whittington. He also looks after the square with Alan Read managing the outfield and worries about the lack of young players coming through and whether the 'friendlies' structure his team prefers has a future.

Horn Fair Day is not only a great social event, it is the club's main fundraiser, although much-appreciated grants are also received from the Parish Council. Little of its income goes to the landlord, as Lord Egremont charges only a small annual peppercorn rent. Hazel Biggs, Jean Stemp and Mandy Morrish provide excellent teas with much-appreciated help from the team's WAGs. They earned the club a very welcome £1,000 when the judges of the 2015 *Daily Telegraph*'s Great Cricket Tea Challenge, including Mike (cricket's answer to Paul Hollywood) Gatting, selected them as runners-up.

Club: Ebernoe C.C.

Elmley Castle

Worcestershire

Elmley Castle has been called one of the Ten Most Beautiful Villages in England. But if you go expecting to find a medieval castle to explore and the local cricket club playing serenely in its grounds, you will be disappointed. The castle, built shortly after the Norman Conquest, fell into disrepair over the centuries and its stones were carted off to build Pershore Bridge and other structures. Elmley Castle Cricket Club, founded in 1854, used to play in its precincts but, according to club President Brian Woodford, the playing surface was "rustic and primitive and on the side of a hill". So in the mid-1950s, the club moved

to the Village Playing Field, known locally as the Turnip Field, because turnips were grown there during World War II.

Woodford's 50-year cricketing career ended a few years back when he was 73. He is proud that recent teams have included as many as nine players who went to the local school, even though, he says, "young people have largely been priced out of the area".

The club resisted playing league cricket for as long as possible but, unable to get Saturday

fixtures, joined the Cotswold Hills League and has worked its way up to Division I. It also runs a Sunday side and three very competitive youth teams, coached by Steve Webb. A weekly barbecue run from April to July does wonders in attracting the youngsters.

Because the ground is managed by the Parish Council, planning permission is needed for any changes, such as replacing the artificial concrete-based net with AstroTurf. Club secretary Robin Eaton also thinks more protection is needed for a couple of bungalows within six-hitting range and

peppered by batsmen over the years. The club used to repair all broken roof tiles, he says, and once erected a 12-foot-high permanent barrier, but the ball still went over. The outfield and seven strips are well-cared-for by groundsman Lance Cooper, a former player, aided by club members and a ride-on roller. The 1960s-era pavilion has been modernised bit by bit, with a pitched roof replacing a flat roof, the installation of a kitchen and upstairs changing rooms.

Brian Woodford says that the club identifies strongly with Worcestershire CCC and remembers when the full county side came to the village to celebrate Elmley Castle's 125th anniversary and Worcestershire player Paul Pridgeon's benefit. He also tells of a vicar of the 1940s who played for the village side. He and his family were so cricket mad that when a son was born, they gave the baby a bat to chew on. The baby grew up to be John Snow, the Sussex and England fast bowler, so that's obviously the way to do it.

Club: Elmley Castle C.C.

Firle

East Sussex

The glory of Firle's cricket ground is its oaks, which surround the playing area two or three deep and give the village its name; 'Firle' comes from the Anglo-Saxon 'fierol' which means 'oak-covered land'. The oaks have certainly seen a lot of cricket over the years. As far back as 1725, the Duke of Richmond, one of early cricket's most important patrons, challenged his friend Sir William Gage, to a two-a-side match at Firle. Sir William, a keen cricketer and owner of Firle Place, was the first importer of a kind of plum which now bears his name – the greengage. In his acceptance letter, he mentioned tongue-in-cheek that he was 'in great affliction' having lost a game the previous day. Sir William must have been even more miserable when he lost to the Duke the following

Tuesday. Given his fondness for cricket, it is possible that Sir William encouraged Firle Cricket Club, which dates its formation to 1758, a few years after his death. Relations between club and the Gage family have always been very amicable. Rental is nominal and the current Viscount Gage is club president.

Firle's square with its twelve strips is maintained by the players under the direction of Lawrence Kemp, the groundsman, using equipment which

RIGHT: An original handbill for the match involving eleven Gentlemen of Firle, with a dinner provided at The Ram Inn.

BELOW: The eleven Gentlemen of Firle playing the eleven Gentlemen of Isfield in less than clement conditions in 2018.

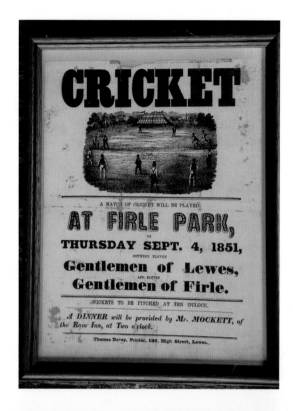

the club admits is not in the first flush of youth. Over the years Firle has run a strong side. It used to play in the Cuckmere Cricket League and won the title 17 times from 1952. Since joining the East Sussex Cricket League in 2007, the Saturday team has shot up the divisions and now plays in Division 2. A midweek eleven plays T20 on a Wednesday, all home games.

Among its opponents are the Gentlemen of Lewes, a very long-standing rivalry dating back to about 1851, according to a poster of that time in the pavilion. The Sunday side's 2017 schedule had fewer matches, but did include the star fixture (or should that be diva fixture), a game against nearby Glyndebourne Opera House, skippered by their executive chairman Gus Christie. His younger brother Tol captains Firle's Sunday XI, for whom Christie also plays regularly.

The beauty of the ground and the village attracts many touring sides. Members of the Bloomsbury group also fell in love with the area and lived in the nearby Charleston Farmhouse. Indeed, Vanessa Bell, sister of Virginia Woolf, her son Quintin, and her lover, Duncan Grant, are buried in the local church, St. Peter's.

BELOW: A photo looking towards the South Downs with Firle Place beyond the cricket ground and St. Peter's church and the village of Firle to the right.

Fulking

West Sussex

Only a few miles from the Regency splendours of Brighton lies the tiny village of Fulking (population 300) with a pub, a memorial to John Ruskin and little else apart from a cricket club. Set in one of the most glorious parts of the South Downs, it's a favourite starting point for walkers eager to enjoy the breathtaking views the countryside has to offer.

In theory, with such a small catchment area, a team might struggle to survive here. Not so with Preston Nomads, thanks to a remarkable cricket enthusiast, Spen Cama. One day in 1937, Spen – then in his late twenties and studying for the bar – drove into the village and discovered that some of its prime real estate was for sale. Spen and some friends had started Preston Nomads ten years earlier. With no ground of its own, the club played on Brighton corporation pitches. Cama, desperate to find a permanent home for the team, thought the meadows in Fulking would be ideal. He bought some of the plots and as time went on, added to them, eventually establishing two grounds, a larger one for the Firsts and Seconds, and a smaller one for Third and Fourth XIs.

Cama led the club as player, chairman and president till his death in 2001, when his will made newspaper headlines. Sussex CCC, whose President Spen had been from 1980 to 1983, received about £12 million and Preston Nomads was the principal beneficiary of a trust fund of several million pounds. The club has spent Spen's bequest wisely. The two adjoining grounds have been substantially upgraded and a striking new flint and brick pavilion constructed, large enough to accommodate the club's very active colts section, as well as the adults. The ground has also become a training area for the next generation of Sussex's groundsmen, which suits everyone: Preston Nomads get an immaculately tended playing area and Sussex well-trained apprentices.

Strong leadership after Spen's death has ensured that Preston Nomads continues to grow. The club, which puts out four Saturday XIs, is very successful and has won many Sussex Premier League and other divisional titles at all levels. In 2009, it won its first national trophy, the ECB Club Indoor Championship at Lord's.

It's hard to say if the Nomads are the richest club in village cricket, but there is no doubt that local cricket is reaping the benefit Spen Cama would have wished.

Club: Preston Nomads C.C.

BELOW: A view from the Downs shows off the impeccable cricket facilities supported by Spen Cama's bequest.

Goodwood

West Sussex

Goodwood and cricket date back to at least 1702 and Goodwood House holds the original of the oldest set of the Laws of Cricket in existence: Lord's only has a copy. But though the ground and club are steeped in cricket history, there is no sense that after 300 years the club is resting on its laurels or that its energy levels are low.

Much of this stems from the continued interest shown by the occupiers of Goodwood House, beginning with the 2nd Duke of Richmond (1701-1750), a grandson of Charles II. In 1727, he and a Mr Alan Brodrick of Peper Harrow Park, near Godalming, raised teams to play each other. As was common in those days, bets were struck. Sixteen rules were agreed in writing – the Laws referred to earlier – to avoid any nasty quibbling over the result.

The 4th Duke (1764-1819), an active cricketer, was a founder member of the MCC and a backer of Thomas Lord, and the 5th Duke (1791-1860), as Earl of March, was President of the MCC. The 10th Duke (1929-2017) took a very keen interest in the game and was President/Patron of Sussex CCC for over 25 years. He played both for and against the club and encouraged the ground's use as a centre of excellence for the development of local cricket for all ages. His son, the 11th Duke, is just as committed.

Cricket is played with the magnificent Regency frontage of Goodwood House as background. The House and grounds are Grade I listed, but the most eye-catching feature is possibly the 100-foot-high (30 metres) Cedar of Lebanon planted in the 1760s marginally outside the boundary. The thatch-roofed pavilion with picket fence, built in 1952 by the estate employees, fits very naturally into its surroundings in front of a grove of mature trees. Teas, catered in turns by players' families, have always been of a very high standard, peaking in 2017 when Mary Berry visited the ground for filming and contributed one of her cakes.

Famous names love to play here, including James Lillywhite (an employee of the Duke), Sir Colin Cowdrey, Ray Lindwall, Ted Dexter and Graham Gooch. A huge amount of cricket is played on the twelve strips. Club games take place on Saturdays and Sundays, and the estates side, drawn from the 700 employees, plays 20/20 on Thursday evenings. In addition, there are corporate friendlies and other matches which are part of the Horse Racing and Motor Revival Festivals. And from 2017, Chichester Priory Park C.C. began to play all its first and second team home matches at Goodwood.

Keeping the ground in the best shape possible is the responsibility of Richard Geffen, the club chairman, who is helped by three colleagues. Richard reckons there are as many as 130 games a season and plans so that no strip is used more than five times. He is grateful for the window from mid-June to mid-July when cricket steps aside to allow the Festival of Speed to take place. That's when cars of all ages, shapes and sizes do their thing and, according to Richard, "the whole area becomes a mini-city of tents, food concessions, picnic areas and people."

Club: Goodwood C.C.

BELOW: The cricket match played during the Goodwood Revival Meeting in September gets a fantastic crowd all dressed in vintage clothing.

BOTTOM: Some slacker taking it easy out on the boundary.

Grassington

North Yorkshire

Upper Wharfedale C.C.'s ground at Wood Lane lies on the edge of the pretty village of Grassington. It is good sheep-rearing country and sturdy dry stone walls are needed to keep the persistent woolly beasts off the pitch, a formidable bunch if the club's aggressive ram's head logo is anything to go by.

Wood Lane is owned by the locally-based Gardner Trust, a philanthropic organisation set up to support local sports activities, which has allowed Upper Wharfedale to play free-of-charge since the club was founded in 1974. The sports centre is a busy place. Three of the local villages play midweek T20 matches on the spacious park and it is also home to rugby teams. The route of the memorable Yorkshire Dales section of the 2014 Tour de France passed nearby.

Upper Wharfedale describes itself as 'The Small Club with a Big Heart' and it has certainly needed that heart during recent difficult periods. After playing in the Airedale and Wharfedale League since 2001, the struggle to raise a second team caused it to withdraw from the league in 2016. Well-advanced plans to build an ambitious new pavilion were one casualty of that decision. "It was very disappointing after so much work had been done," says chairman Jon Slater, "but it was the only sensible decision. Instead, we gave our existing pavilion a good upgrade from the kitchen through to the toilets and it's done the trick!"

The club is sailing in clearer waters now after joining the Nidderdale League in 2017. "We were kindly allowed to enter at Division 6 level, rather than at the bottom, Division 8. We had a highly successful first season and won every game, as well as one of the cup competitions, and we've got our eyes set on a few more promotions." Behind this renewed optimism is an excellent youth set-up with over 100 juniors, and teams ranging from the U-9s to the U-17s. "Very talented players are graduating to the senior sides," says Slater. "What's really satisfying is that 100% of the first team have come up via the youth system. They stay because they love playing at this stunning ground. When the wind sweeps across the moors, Wood Lane can be bleak and finger-numbing, but on a good day, it can be the most beautiful place in the world to play."

Club: Upper Wharfedale C.C.

BELOW: Upper Wharfedale C.C. batting against Knaresborough Forest C.C. Second XI.

Great Budworth

Cheshire

The story behind the creation of Great Budworth C.C. in 2006 is one of great local enthusiasm and energy, underpinned by the generous support of a patron willing to make the grounds of his estate available to the community.

Arley Hall, where the club plays, is an attractive Cheshire country house not far from the village. Home to Viscount Ashbrook and his family, the estate and gardens have won many awards and appeared as backdrops for several TV series such as *The Forsyte Saga* and two wedding scenes in *Coronation Street*. Lord Ashbrook's son, Rowland Flower, is the club's president.

There has been a cricket facility on the estate, including a sturdy, timber-clad pavilion, since 1902. It was built so that one of the family, who was captain of cricket at Eton, could invite friends down for a weekend game. Later, Arley C.C. played here until its demise in the 1980s, when cricket ceased and the ground suffered from lack of attention.

That might have marked the end of cricket in the village, but in 2004, the vicar, the Reverend Alec Brown, initiated one-off matches against nearby Antrobus and Pickmere, which were repeated the following summer. By now, Great Budworth had got the taste for the summer game and via the Vicar's contacts with Lord Ashbrook were offered the chance to play a full summer's schedule at Arley Hall if they could raise the finance.

The village pulled together in such a remarkable way that the club soon had 80 members and the funds were raised in short order. "The level of support is amazing, even from members who aren't cricket fans," says club chairman and groundsman Peter McAndrew. "Two years ago, we raised £10,000 at an auction and bought a decent mower and three pitch covers, as we were losing a lot of time to the weather. And we had a bit of a windfall when we received a £2,000 community grant because we're under the flight path of Manchester Airport!"

The club runs just the one team which plays Saturday or Sunday friendlies and there is also a midweek T20 side. They don't do much travelling as opponents insist on playing at beautiful Arley Hall. The 1902 pavilion is still in place and hasn't been significantly upgraded, but when one of your team is MD of a brewery in Manchester, there are some compensations.

Club: Great Budworth C.C.

Hagley Hall

Worcestershire

It is no surprise to find a thriving cricket club at Hagley Hall. The Grade-I listed neo-Palladian house, near Birmingham, is home to the Lytteltons – a passionate cricketing family which has produced several first-class players. In the 1860s, the family had so many active young cricketers that it took on nearby Bromsgrove School and beat them by 10 wickets. The best known is probably the Hon. Alfred Lyttelton. The original all-rounder, he gained Blues in five different sports, won an England soccer cap, and was England's wicket-keeper in the famous 1882 Test at the Oval which gave birth to The Ashes. In time, he became President of the MCC and a cabinet minister.

Hagley C.C. was formed in 1834 and plays on the Green in front of the The Hall and neighbouring St. John Baptist church. At one time, cows grazed in the outfield, but these days peacocks and geese from the Hall wander onto the playing area. It is a typically spacious tranquil English cricket setting.

Hagley, which has won several divisional titles, runs three Saturday sides in the Worcestershire County League and has a strong junior section in which girls are encouraged to take part. It's

had several generations of pavilions, starting in 1886 with a wooden house built on wheels so it could be moved away and stored at the end of the season. The current 1954 pavilion has been extended over the years. Ground management is undertaken by David Hill, who has been with Hagley since he was a lad of 10 and filled virtually every position of significance in the club, and by Mark Baker, who also looks after the club's second ground in nearby Blakedown.

Relations with the Hall are very amiable. The club pays only a peppercorn rent and Viscount Cobham, who played for Hagley in his day, makes the Hall available for important club events such as its 175th Anniversary in 2009. Three hundred guests attended and speakers included Graham Gooch and Jeremy Coney. The Hon. Alfred would no doubt have been highly gratified, but possibly not the jazz musician Humphrey, who once slipped away from the Eton-Harrow game to buy his first trumpet.

Club: Hagley C.C.

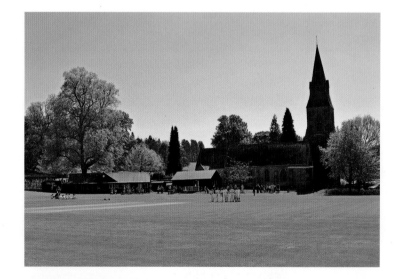

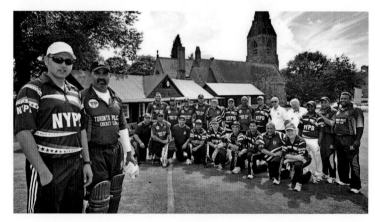

RIGHT: In 2015 as part of the Hagley Cricket Carnival, the ground hosted a very unusual game between the NYPD cricket team and the Toronto Police cricket team. Toronto won with a ball to spare.

Haworth

Yorkshire

These days Haworth, the centre of Bronte Country, supports just the one village side. But there was a time in the 1890s when the *Keighley News* match reports covered no fewer than seven Haworth teams. Many were attached to local churches. Haworth C.C. itself began life in 1887 as Haworth Wesleyans, then became Haworth Methodists, adopting its present name only in 1992. One by one over the years, all the other clubs have disappeared, most recently Haworth West End in 2015 (though their ground is still rented out).

West Lane – the club's home since 1951 – is a small ground, only 80 by 70 yards, so sixes are quite common. Hewn out of a sloping hillside, it commands sweeping views over the Worth Valley with the Pennines visible to the west. According to long-time committee member, Kath Gower, the old joke, 'if you can see the hills, it's about to rain and if you can't, it already is' has more than a grain of truth. On certain days, water pours down the slope, despite the £50,000 of drainage improvements, funded by Sport England. But Kath Gower is keen to add the upside: "On a summer's day it's a glorious place to be!"

The club runs two Saturday sides in the Craven & District League. In recent years the Firsts have held their own in the top Division, winning the Championship for the only time so far in 2012 – a wonderful way to celebrate the club's 125th anniversary year.

Haworth faces the future with confidence, safe in the knowledge that it owns its West Lane ground. The club is prudent in the best Yorkshire sense and makes sure it balances the books. In 2011, a £10,000 grant from The Big Lottery Fund part-financed a clubroom extension and a new £16,000 LED scorebox was paid for out of the club's own funds in 2017. Always looking for other sources of income, the club shrewdly benefits from the Bronte and Haworth effect. When the village is invaded by aficionados for the extremely popular Haworth 1940s Weekend and parking space is at a premium, club volunteers turn the ground into a car park and the moneys raised all go towards the next club project – thank you very much!

Club: Haworth C.C.

RIGHT: A Haworth batsman plays straight from the MCC textbook in their home game versus Crossflats C.C. in the Craven & District League.

Holkham Hall

Norfolk

Holkham Hall, constructed in the 18th century and home to the Earls of Leicester, is located not far from the North Norfolk Heritage coast. Cricket has been played in this magnificent setting since the 1840s when the 2nd Earl levelled part of the Deer Park to make a square. Eventually up to 60 matches a year were played. In the 1920s, one of his successors went a stage further and arranged for the square to be relaid by groundsmen from Lord's.

These days the ground is used by three teams. The estates plays a handful of matches, including games against other estates such as Sandringham House and Houghton Hall. The Nubian Ostriches is an occasional side made up of the Earl's friends who sometimes arrive by helicopter. The bulk of the cricket is played by Holkham C.C., for whom the Earl, who is life president of the club, makes occasional appearances.

Holkham runs just the one side and plays only friendlies. With opponents, such as the Eton Ramblers and Lincolnshire Poachers, more than happy to play in such classic surroundings, almost all the games are at home.

Up to a couple of years ago, the pavilion was an ageing structure, described as a 'quaint shed', with no electricity, a very basic kitchen and no facilities. But all that changed when the estate commissioned a new pavilion, opened in 2017. It is a graceful yet discreet timber-framed building which the architects modelled on cricket pavilions of the late 19th century, 'the heyday of country house cricket and cricket at Holkham'. Sited besides a clump of oaks, the new clubhouse sits very comfortably in the same landscape as the Palladian-style Holkham Hall and was Highly Commended in The Georgian Group's Architectural Awards 2017. Occasional visits by stags and deer add to the charm.

Another glory of the ground is the mouthwatering teas. Prepared by the estate in its café, delicacies such as crayfish tail sandwiches and an irresistible array of gateaus are enough to slow down any cricketer. 'Field *before* tea' is probably the best advice.

RIGHT: Looking from the Hall end towards the 120-foot (36.5 metre) Thomas Coke Monument built between 1845-1848.

Honley

Yorkshire

When Jonathan Rice ran the rule over the Honley pavilion in *The Pavilion Book of Pavilions* in 1991, he said it looked like 'a Chinese pagoda from the outside and the aftermath of a Vicarage Bring and Buy sale on the inside'. The upstairs basins were 'probably more interesting as antiques than as things for washing in...' One gets the picture. The club took the hint and in 2017 a magnificent new upgrade was unveiled. Admittedly it had taken 25 years, but this is cricket, one shouldn't rush these things. Club chairman Rob Moore admits, "The pavilion was falling to pieces. It was definitely dangerous."

The pagoda started life as a single-storey wooden building in the 1890s. Only when the second storey was added in the 1930s did the oriental resemblance emerge. An extension was added after the War to house a tea room and bar.

Now, with a splendid new second wing and the complete refurbishment of the original pavilion, Honley has a clubhouse worthy of its cricketing achievements. A magnificent £350,000 was raised for the project, a real community effort backed by ECB funding.

Although it took the club 125 years to win its first Huddersfield League title in 2005, once started it couldn't stop and has now won many titles and

cups in all the major competitions. With over 140 juniors, Honley has a thriving youth section. A barbecue on training nights each Friday tempts along both young players and their parents. The ground – held in trust for the people of Honley – looks immaculate and is a popular venue for Yorkshire U-19s and the MCC.

The club's professionals have included top-class players such as Craig White, Arnie Sidebottom and Steve Crook. But the club's favourite son is undoubtedly Alonzo Drake. Born in 1884, Drake excelled at both cricket and football and played for Honley before joining Yorkshire in 1909. His outstanding achievement was probably taking all 10 wickets in the innings against Somerset in the space of just 42 balls with match figures of 15 for 51. Drake, who tragically died aged only 35, lived most of his short life in Honley. His memory is perpetuated in the club's logo through the symbol of a water fowl: not a duck but, happily, a drake.

Club: Honley C.C.

Hovingham

North Yorkshire

Although many clubs have strong connections to stately homes – Blenheim Palace, Goodwood House and Belvoir Castle to name but three – nowhere are the ties between club and landlord stronger than at Hovingham Hall, home of the Worsley family.

The history of cricket at the Hall goes back a long way. Games have certainly been played here since the 1820s, and a photograph exists of a match in 1858, the year a 22-strong Hovingham side took on an All-England XI and lost.

The Worsleys have lived at Hovingham Hall since 1563. The family's ties with cricket, and with Yorkshire CCC in particular, were probably strongest during the lifetime of the 4th Baronet, Sir William Worsley (1890-1973). Sir William, a good amateur, played first-class cricket for two years when he was in his late thirties, captaining Yorkshire to fourth position in the County Championship in 1928 and third in 1929. He lost only two games, a creditable record if he hadn't finished behind Lancashire in both seasons. He also served as President of the club for 13 years and as President of the MCC.

Unsurprisingly, many well-known Yorkshire cricketers have played at Hovingham, including Wilfred Rhodes, Herbert Sutcliffe, Hedley Verity, Fred Trueman and Geoffrey Boycott, and the venue has often been used for benefit matches. The club runs two teams in the York Senior League Galtres division – the name comes from an ancient forest north of York. Home games are played on what is effectively the front lawn of this Grade I-listed mansion. The unprotected windows look temptingly within cow-shot range but are rarely hit. A few years back David Prest hit a small top window and was awarded £5 by Sir Marcus Worsley (1925-2012), which was the going rate set by his father, the 4th Baronet.

The club maintains the playing area and ten strips and Stuart Prest, the chairman, is full of praise for Dave Skilbeck, groundsman since 1990, who won Best Groundsman in the Yorkshire League in 2016. No doubt Dave would sympathise with the equipment used by his 19th-century and early 20th-century predecessors. According to the daughter of the 3rd Baronet, Victoria King-Farlow, "In those days, the pitch was mown by a horse-drawn mower, the horse wearing boots, and rolled by a large water-filled roller with shafts, usually pulled by hefty men." There were also "three-feet-high iron railings around the boundary, which presented a danger to the fielders." The pavilion used to be a converted World War II hut, but the club raised £73,000 for a more modern replacement which was opened in 2009.

Club: Hovingham C.C.

RIGHT AND BELOW: Photos taken at Hovingham during their match against Sessay in 2017. Sessay brought along their Yorkshire Girls' U-15 wicket-keeper to act as scorer.

Ickwell Green

Bedfordshire

The old lime tree that used to lie within the boundary at Kent County Cricket Ground in Canterbury was not unique in English cricket. In the process of compiling this book it's been found that many village clubs have trees within the boundary ropes, including Southborough in Kent, which has two, and variable rules depending on which of the magnificent specimens you hit. At Knole Park there is a tree substantially inside the playing area.

However none can have a tree as far into the playing area as Ickwell Green near Biggleswade in Bedfordshire. Their magnificent 260-year-old oak, emblazoned on the club badge, is a full 13 paces inside the marked boundary. The lower branches of this arboricultural beauty are just 22 paces from the edge of the square. Furthermore, should one wish to watch the game from under the shade of its spreading branches, there is a bench seat placed there. On match days, to separate spectators from the playing area a white line encircles the bench and like many other clubs, any shot that hits the tree is signalled a four. Gerry Ingham, who has played for many years says the tree is rarely hit: "In fact it is not unusual for there to be no 'hits' throughout an entire game. It appears as if the tree exudes a powerful magnetic field that deflects the ball around its bulk."

Cricket has been played on Ickwell Green since 1839 and it is still surrounded by thatched cottages. Indeed, a vintage photo of a match in progress in 1955 shows a hayrick, a thatched pavilion and the Ickwell oak outside of the boundary with bicycles parked underneath. It is clearly a village that values tradition — at the time of photography in late April, a May pole was being prepared across the road.

It's a very active cricket club with First and Second XIs who play Saturday cricket in Divisions 2 and 4 of the Huntingdonshire County Cricket League. Switching counties, on Sundays they play in Divisions 1 and 4 of the Bedfordshire County League. They take part in local midweek cup competitions, such as the East Bedfordshire Charity Heritage Cup and Senior Shield, and the East Beds under-18 competition.

Club: Ickwell C.C.

TOP: A view of the old thatched pavilion in 1955 by George Skevington of the *Biggleswade Chronicle*. The fielding position in font of the tree is known as "tree patrol" not extra cover.

RIGHT: White flags mark the boundary and show how far inside the oak is located.

Instow

North Devon

On a day of gentle summer breezes and sparkling views across the Taw and Torridge estuaries, North Devon C.C.'s ground in Instow can be distractingly beautiful.

A local newspaper clipping framed in the ancient pavilion tells the story of the North Devon club and its arrival at the 6-acre site on the coast. The club was formed in Barnstaple in 1823 but moved to Instow in 1832 and made use of a large thatched barn as its pavilion. Though the exact date of the barn is not known, it is thought to have been built no later than 1760, making it one of the oldest pavilions in the country, if not the oldest.

The ground looks immaculate because the club sets itself high standards and employs a full-time professional groundsman during the summer. Andrew Cameron, described as "a superb groundsman", has been in the job for 20 years and produces what the club thinks is "the best all-round playing area in Devon", even though he has to produce pitches for something like 100 games a year, including Minor Counties games.

North Devon has had particular success with youth sides over the years and you don't have to wait very long before the names of Craig and Mark Overton are casually dropped into the conversation. Both played for the club till

their late teens before moving on to Somerset. Their father Mark, together with Jan Witheridge, coaches the club's ladies side, North Devon Tarka Ladies, which won the top division of the Devon Women's Cricket League in 2016 and 2017.

Another great name associated with the club is David Shepherd, the former Gloucestershire

BELOW: The club flag stands stiffly in the onshore breeze. Bowling from the pavilion end in these conditions is a lot more work than bowling from the dunes end.

player, who went on to stand as an umpire in 92 Tests. Shepherd spent his retirement years in Instow, occasionally working in the local post office run by his brother Bill, and he often came to watch the games. When he died in 2009, his ashes were spread on the ground.

A curiosity is the scorer's box which looks innocent enough, but is in fact a converted World War II blockhouse, embellished to look innocently rustic. The blockhouse is a Listed building, as is the pavilion, which has no solid roof, simply a covering of thatch supported by beams. It's the kind of place you could well imagine David Shepherd seeing out his days.

Club: North Devon C.C.

ABOVE: A view across the Torridge estuary to Appledore.

RIGHT: The interior of the circa-1760 barn that became the cricket club pavilion, possibly Britain's oldest building used for such a purpose.

Keswick

Cumbria

With the imposing fells of Skiddaw, Latrigg and Helvellyn as a backdrop and flanked by the River Greta, not many grounds have such imposing and picturesque surroundings as Fitz Park. The spectacular setting earned Keswick C.C. the title of Loveliest Ground in the Country in a competition run by *Wisden Cricket Monthly* in 2001.

Cricket has been played at Fitz Park since the 1880s and its long-term future is protected by the terms of the Park Trust. On serene days, visitors enjoy the wonderful summer evenings and gorgeous views. But in December 2015, the club suffered the catastrophe of Storm Desmond. The river overflowed its banks and the ground was flooded for the first time in its history. "Seven hundred tonnes of silt were eventually removed," says club chairman Keith Richardson, "and the recently-upgraded pavilion with Victorian wooden framework had to be totally refurbished."

It was a devastating blow, but thanks to much hard work by the club members and with financial assistance from the ECB, the ground was ready for the start of the 2016 season. Keith Richardson was named UK Chairman of the Year by *All Out Cricket* for his efforts. Keswick still won a creditable eight games and remained in the Premier Division of the North Lancs and Cumbria Cricket League. Former England captain Mike Gatting officially reopened the ground in August 2016, although bad weather again intervened and the celebration match against Cleator was cancelled. It was another difficult year in 2017 with nine of the 21 matches abandoned. Match reports described the run-ups as 'like a paddy field'. The club won only three games all season and narrowly avoided relegation.

Keswick runs three Saturday sides and various age-group junior teams and plays rent-free. However it is responsible for the upkeep of pavilion and the ground, which is kept to a high standard and has hosted minor counties fixtures in the past. Famous visitors have included Darren Gough, Hansie Cronje and David Boon.

The club is committed to developing cricket locally and the club professional Geeth Kumara coaches students from the town's local comprehensive school. Women's cricket is thriving with weekly practice sessions on the ground and over 50 women take part in the highly popular Women's Cricket Festival day. The club also stages tournaments for the blind and partially sighted.

Club: Keswick C.C.

Kildale

North Yorkshire

Mentioned in the Domesday Book and with village boundaries that haven't changed in 900 years, Kildale is a tiny community in the north-west of the North York Moors National Park which gives off a sense of dogged permanence. The village is part of an ancient estate owned by the Turton-Sutcliffe family for almost 200 years. The current head of the family, Andrew Sutcliffe QC, used to play for Kildale and is now its president.

The club is one of a number of cricketing communities dotted about the vast expanse of the moors. Formed in 1902, Kildale played only friendlies at first, but in 1953 joined the Langbaurgh League, becoming one of the most successful sides. Every time it tops the league, Andrew Sutcliffe treats the team to a celebratory dinner in the village hall.

The club runs two sides – a Saturday team in the Langbaurgh League and a Wednesday T20 side in the Esk Valley Evening League.

The club has a strong spine of local families such as the Doughtys, the Peirsons and the Cooks. Dave Doughty, the secretary, and Michael Peirson share the groundskeeping duties. Before

them, the late Alan Peirson contributed yeoman service as player, secretary, treasurer and groundsman for over 50 years. Another member of the Cook family, Dave, is club umpire. "I don't play favourites," he says. "I give LBWs, family or no family," but so far it's always been slipping down legside.

Club: Kildale C.C.

Kinross

Kinross-shire

The Kinross-based cricket club has had a roundabout journey before settling at its spacious ground on the banks of Loch Leven. Founded in 1855, it moved several times before transferring in 1991 to the council-owned Myre Park, playing on an artificial pitch wedged between football pitches.

At this point, the club's profile was not particularly high, but in 2004 a new management team took control, which decided to establish a junior section for primary and secondary school children. Three first team players were sent on Cricket Scotland coaching courses and by the next season a full coaching programme was under way, helped by the Lord's Taverner's' donation of a bag of junior coaching equipment.

With the numbers of children growing rapidly,

more space was needed and in 2007 the club moved to the beautiful, 17th-century Kinross House overlooking the Loch. It wasn't long before the men's and boys' sides were winning trophies and in 2009 Kinross-shire was named the *Wisden Cricketer* 'Club of the Year.' The relatively new Women's and Girls' teams performed every bit as well with the Women's side winning two major titles in 2010. The same season, the senior men won Division I of the Strathmore and Perthshire League for the third consecutive year.

At this high point, Kinross House was suddenly sold, meaning the club needed a new ground for the 2012 season. Despite all its efforts, it was unsuccessful and was forced to play all its home matches away. Then the cricketing equivalent of a miracle happened. Rob Niven, a cricket-loving

local farmer, owned land on the banks of Loch Leven, which was too small and oddly-shaped for farming. He offered the space to the club, which gratefully accepted.

Kinross-shire feels it has looked into the abyss and bounced back. According to club captain, secretary and groundsman John Ross, it loves its new location which is full of interesting wildlife and varieties of trees. It has a 100-year lease and pays a hardly-extortionate £100 annual rental. Mr. Niven even cuts the outfield for them. The new wood-cladded pavilion is a Portakabin which the club has extended and enhanced with a balustrade carved to look like bats and stumps shattered by a ball.

Recent experiences have changed the club, according to John Ross. "We're more focussed on the community now. Our coaches work with primary schools throughout the county, which is why we call ourselves Kinross-shire, rather than Kinross. There are lots of lonely and elderly folk in the area and we're buying gazebos so they can come and watch the cricket in our beautiful ground. Another feature is Rob Niven's restaurant Loch Leven's Larder on the farm. It's a great place to go after a match and nice that we can show our appreciation for what we owe him and have a good meal at the same time."

Club: Kinross-shire C.C.

Knightshayes Court

Bolham, Devon

Heathcoat C.C.'s immaculate ground overlooks the lush Exe valley in Devon. It is part of the National Trust's Knightshayes Court estate, and very much wrapped up in the Heathcoat-Amory family history.

John Heathcoat was an inventor and designed and patented a machine that revolutionised the production of lace. After his machines in Loughborough were destroyed by Luddites he moved his manufacturing to Tiverton in Devon. His descendant Sir John Heathcoat-Amory, 1st Baronet, is said to have chosen the site of Knightshayes because from the site Sir John could see his factory in the distance, nestled in the Exe valley below. The grand Gothic Revival building was completed in 1874.

His son, H. H. Amory was a prominent batsman with the local village team Bolham C.C. and a scorebook covering the years 1889 to 1894 shows this to be the club from which Heathcoat Cricket Club arose. The Amory family were a major source of players and in 1921 the club formally became known as Heathcoat C.C. A pitch was established within the estate grounds, gaining the iron railings that still surround the ground and a large pavilion that preceded the current edifice. Prior to that the pavilion had been a cramped log cabin with a thatched roof, with such small dimensions that tea had to be taken in an adjoining marquee.

During the World War II Knightshayes was used for a time as a convalescent home for the U.S. Eighth Air Force and was eventually bought by the National Trust in 1972, however the team has continued in its current home suffering the fluctuations of promotions and relegations in the leagues (although one was apparently by a clerical error).

Today the club has a thriving junior section; there are two teams in the Tolchards Devon League and eight junior teams, including U-10 and U13 girls sides. The facilities of the club are first class, not least the new pavilion built in 2013 and a playing surface of billiard table quality.

Club: Heathcoat C.C. (twinned with Heathcote C.C. New Zealand)

Knole Park

Sevenoaks, Kent

If you like your cricket with occasional intrusions by fallow deer, you will be charmed by Knole Park, the home of Sennocke C.C. The name is a contraction of Seven Oaks and the final letter 'e' is sounded. Knole is one of the last remaining medieval deer parks in the country and the animals have right of way, both on the park road and the playing area. If they like the look of the grass at wide mid-off, you have to be patient till they move on.

Less animate is the prominent pine tree in the outfield, conspicuous in 18th-century prints and easily reachable by aggressive batting. A shot striking the tree is worth four, whether full toss or on the bounce. Occasionally, a ball thrown in wildly from the outfield will stick in the branches. It can be dislodged by hitting it with another ball, but this has been known to take 20 minutes. Requests from locals that their ashes are spread beneath the tree are not unknown (but not encouraged during games).

With buildings straight out of the Middle Ages edging the boundary, it must be hard sometimes for the cricketers to know which century they are playing in. The property was acquired by the National Trust in 1946 but the Sackville family, which has lived there since 1604, remains a very strong presence. A highlight of the season is the annual match between the club and a side got up by the 7th Baron, Robert Sackville-West.

Cricket runs very strongly in Sackville veins. Lord John Sackville, son of the 1st Duke of Dorset (1688-1765), became captain of Kent in 1735. The 3rd Duke, also a John Sackville (1745-1799), was a good player, an important patron of cricket and a founder member of the MCC. He gave the Vine Cricket Ground – then part of the Knole estate and now sandwiched between two busy roads – to the town of Sevenoaks for the annual rent of one peppercorn, doubled to two when a pavilion was added. The town must also pay each Lord Sackville one cricket ball a year (if asked). The current Lord Sackville plays in the annual game and, when he is batting, it is said that the team's catching becomes less sharp and lbw appeals are non-existent. After the game, the club is invited into the house for refreshments.

Another famous member of the family, the writer Vita Sackville-West, has a tree named after her on the ground, Vita's Tree.

While cricket has been played at Knole Park since the early 18th century, the forerunner of Sennocke C.C. was only formed in 1942 to provide wartime recreation for the local Civil Defence Club. With no ground of its own, in 1948 the club approached Lord Sackville who gave permission for it to play at Knole Park. The last team to play there had been the Knole Estate side before the war, but according to a club history by R. Cheeseman, a Sennocke stalwart for many decades, 'it had become terribly overgrown and covered with molehills…and littered with blockades, set up during the war to stop enemy aircraft from landing.' No longer.

The club runs one Saturday side which plays in the Kent County Village League, but has no junior sections. It doesn't have a formal pavilion either. Teams change in what was once a dungeon, possibly the setting for a painting by Sir Joshua Reynolds on display in the Main House, *Count Ugolino and his Children in the Dungeon*.

Club: Sennocke C.C.

Leigh

Kent

In Leigh – pronounced lie as in the alkaline solution, not Leigh as in Vivien – all roads lead to the Green, an impressively large expanse for such a comparatively small village of less than 2,000 souls.

The Green has been home to Leigh Cricket Club for over 300 years (except on Leigh Fair Day – see below). The year 1700 figures prominently on Leigh's flag and team cap, although the club is convinced that cricket must have been played here decades earlier.

The ground is generously fringed by oaks and horse chestnut trees with one of the oaks famous for being hollow and about 400 years old. The Green is owned by the Parish Council, but the nine pitches are maintained by the club and the outfield by Kent County Council. Perennial drainage problems were solved thanks to a £70,000 grant from Sport England.

Leigh runs two teams on a Saturday in the Kent County Village League, of which they were a founder member, a Sunday XI and a midweek team. A big rival used to be Southborough although they now play in different leagues. When these teams met, a remarkable combined total of over 500 years of cricket history took the field.

The club cannot be accused of splashing out recklessly on pavilions. The first, built in 1896, cost £35 and wasn't replaced till 1972 by the current sturdy, serviceable construction which may well last as long as its predecessor.

Leigh has proud associations with some famous cricketing names. In the early 19th century, family members of the famous cricket ball manufacturers, Duke & Son, still a noted brand, played for the club. One of the team's characters was Isaac 'Ike' Ingrams (1855 -1947) a good innings, as they say. Ike worked for Duke and played for the village team as an excellent wicket-keeper and then for Kent. Brooker is another famous Leigh name, the family once contributing six players to a team to the confusion of the opposition's scorer.

The Kent and England captain Sir Colin Cowdrey occasionally coached the colts team, and the former Australian Test player, John Inverarity, played for the club when a master at nearby Tonbridge school in the 1970s. A long-lasting link with a local pub The Bat and Ball, dating back to 1762, came to an end when the pub closed in 2010.

Although one of the highlights of the cricket year in the 18th and 19th centuries was the game on Leigh Fair Day, the Fair's tea tents, stalls and obstacle races now spread themselves over much of the Green and home matches switch to a neighbouring ground should dates clash. In the late 1790s, you would have seen wax figures of Louis XVI and his wife Marie Antoinette on show only a few years after their execution in the French Revolution, displayed by a French entrepreneuse called Madame Tussaud. Now whatever became of that enterprise?

Club: Leigh C.C.

Linkenholt

Hampshire

Early in the summer of 1946, 14-year-old Elsie Stockley took the bus from Linkenholt into Andover a few miles away. Village cricket was resuming after the War and one of her brothers, John, was the new captain of the village side. Elsie, who was not short of initiative, had volunteered to buy the cakes for the tea interval, not an easy task in those days of rationing. She finally managed to source some, earning herself the grateful thanks of the club and the permanent job of tea lady. Today, if you ask Elsie how she managed it, she will give you a little grin and say, "black market, of course!"

In due course, Elsie married Ray Smith, naturally a keen Linkenholt player. She is now 84, and has done virtually every job at the club, including scorer, pavilion cleaner and fixtures secretary, which she still is. She hasn't been chairman because she never wanted to be.

Elsie can recall players, matches and individual incidents as though they happened yesterday. She still prepares the teas, helped by her sister-in-law Doris Stockley. Her 70 years involvement with the village side was celebrated with a party and presentation in front of the pavilion in 2016.

The pinkish flint from which most of the buildings are constructed gives Linkenholt a mellow rustic atmosphere. With only 30 houses and just over 50 inhabitants, it is almost certainly the smallest village in the book with its own cricket club. There are no shops and the nearest pub is two villages away. In fact, although there is no way of telling, the whole village, except for the church, is part of the 2000-acre Linkenholt estate which has been privately owned since the Dissolution of the Monasteries. Previous owners have regarded the cricket club as an asset well worth preserving, and the current owner, a Swedish businessman, continues that amiable relationship.

The side was founded in 1900 and run by the local postmaster. When he died, Elsie's four brothers rescued the equipment and kept the club running. For a long time the side comprised local villagers who worked on the estate, but more recently the team has been drawn from surrounding villages. The club competed in the Hampshire cricket leagues for many years but now plays Sunday friendlies against local villages and midweek T20. A local farmer, Mark Melly, cuts the outfield and the members and players look after the square and its eight strips. The pavilion, which started life as a reading room in 1900, is bright and comfortable. The well-fitted kitchen also caters for wedding receptions and the shooting parties run by the estate.

Linkenholt's cricket highlights include bowling out local rivals Chute for 3, a match against Southampton F.C., and the occasion when Elsie's brother Frank got struck by a ball which hit the matches in his pocket and set his trousers on fire.

Club: Linkenholt C·C.

TOP RIGHT: The beautiful Grade-II listed church of St. Peter in Linkenholt.

OPPOSITE: Linkenholt C.C. celebrate Elsie Smith's 70-year involvement with the club in 2016.

Longparish

Hampshire

Longparish is a village in Hampshire whose name describes itself. Made up of four hamlets, Forton, Middleton, West Aston and East Aston that straggle along two miles of the B4303, it is indeed a long parish. At one end is the village hall and St. Nicholas Church, at the other a very important location, The Cricketers Inn.

The club was founded in 1874 and for some years games were played in the grounds of Middleton House, the ancient estate across the road from the current club. A cricket ground is visible on the 1911 Ordnance Survey map and after the estate was bought in 1925 by Captain A. S. Wills, cricket was transferred to its current location, also owned and generously donated by the Wills family.

Apart from its Thomas Hardy-esque thatched barn of a pavilion, Longparish's greatest claim to fame has been two appearances in the National Village Cricket final at Lord's. In 1980 they played Marchwiel of North Wales and lost, but in 1987 they beat Yorkshire champions Treeton Welfare to take the top prize.

They currently run three teams in the Hampshire League, a First, Second and Third XI and a Midweek XI playing 20 overs cricket. It's more difficult than ever assembling sides for matches, but at least they have had more success than local rivals Hurstbourne Priors. A couple of miles the other side of The Cricketers pub, this quintessential venue for English cricket has folded through lack of players.

Club: Longparish C.C.

OPPOSITE: Cricket journalist John Woodcock, dubbed "the Sage of Longparish", has an enduring association with Longparish C.C. He was born in the village and retired there after a long and distinguished career working as Cricket Correspondent for *The Times* from 1954 to 1988 and editor of *Wisden* from 1981 to 1986.

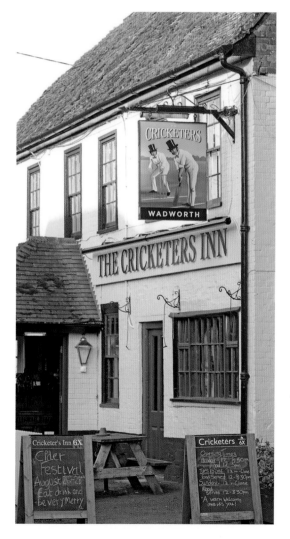

Luddendenfoot

Yorkshire

Based in the hotbed of Yorkshire league cricket centred round Halifax, the club has several identities: Luddendenfoot C.C., in its formal moments; Ludd Foot, when among friends; or simply Foot or #UTF (Up The Foot!) on social media.

Ludd Foot – if one may presume – started life in the 1880s with a much longer name: Luddendenfoot St. Mary's. The link with the parish church meant no-one could play for the team unless they were a member of the church. It wasn't till 1956 that a general meeting authorised the break with the church, thus allowing the club to change its name and permit unrestricted membership.

After moving several times, the club settled at High Lea Green on the edge of the town in the late 1940s. The ground, leased from a local farmer, overlooks the Upper Calder valley and the moors, which look benign enough on a calm summer's day, even if the metal structures supporting the sightscreens are a reminder that the weather can quickly turn blustery.

After re-laying the square and with the opening of a new pavilion, cricket was able to restart in 1950, although the outfield wasn't finally levelled and reseeded till 1953. Even then, a cash crisis almost forced the club to abandon the ground in 1956. Within a couple of years, however, finances were stable enough to buy a new motor cutter and other equipment.

Ludd Foot played in several leagues before joining the Halifax Cricket League in 1973. A few years ago it merged with another local team, King Cross, and has benefited from the influx of new faces. It now runs two Saturday XIs, a Sunday side and four junior teams. Several juniors have graduated to the senior sides and the club is well positioned for the future.

Over the years, the club has continued to develop its facilities. The pavilion was extended in 1997 with the help of a grant, celebrated with a match between a Past & Present XI of the club and a Calder Valley XI. Ludd Foot's ambitions include promotion to the Premier League and further improvements to the clubhouse and practice facilities. What else can one say but UTF!

Club: Luddendenfoot C.C.

BELOW: Walking around the boundary, a visitor will find a memorial stone engraved with a bat and ball. This is a poignant tribute to a young cricketer who played for the club and died aged just 13.

Lurgashall

West Sussex

Lurgashall C.C. plays in a village setting of exceptional tranquillity and beauty in the South Downs National Park in West Sussex. Nothing seems to have changed for generations, which may well be the case, as no fewer than nine local buildings are listed, including the village inn dating from 1557. Known as The Noah's Ark, it is handily located adjacent to the pavilion and earned its slightly unusual name from patrons once having to cross a pond to get to the refreshments – not exactly a flood of biblical proportions, but certainly an inconvenience.

The club suspects its history dates back to the early part of the 19th century. But with the parish priest making a bonfire of all the village records, including the cricket club's, about fifty years ago, it's hard to be certain. It does possess a framed extract from the *West Sussex Gazette* of 1863 recording a match against the neighbouring village of Ebernoe, 'the auld enemy'. The intensity of an Ashes series is nothing compared to the serious business when Ebernoe and Lurgashall meet. Rivalry reaches its peak if the clubs contest the Ebernoe Horn Fair match held each July. The highest-scoring batsman of the winning team is awarded the horns of a barbecued ram presented by Lord Egremont, who lives at nearby Petworth House and is landlord of both clubs.

The club runs just the one team which plays in the I'Anson League. Formed in 1901, it is said to be the oldest continuously-operating village cricket league in the country. Only villages within 12 miles of Grayshott are eligible for membership. Lurgashall made it into the top division in 2017, but once the cricket and football seasons started to overlap, had difficulties raising a team and withdrew. The club also runs a six-a-side tournament on the first Sunday in July each year and makes the ground available to Haslemere's Third XI for its I'Anson fixtures.

Lurgashall is keen to modernise its pavilion, a blacksmith's forge dating from the 19th century. It will cost £12,000 but the club is confident the funds can be raised. The quality of the square and nine strips, managed by Rob Dale, earns much deserved praise. Rob provides all the equipment, although the club does admit to possessing a 1938 roller.

Like Napoleon's army, a cricket team marches on its stomach and the club's motto, prominent on the home page, is 'Home of the best cricket teas around'. It owes its excellent refreshments to the tasty sandwiches and cakes made by the club's tea ladies, Rose Dillon-Thiselton and Nicky Clark. They follow in the footsteps of tea lady extraordinaire Jacqui Lawson, who initiated The Great Tea Ladies Strike of 1976. Tired of having to wash up the crockery in cold water, she decided to serve tea using paper plates and cups. The men soon capitulated and she got her hot water.

Club: Lurgashall C.C.

133

Lustleigh

Devon

One glance at the fixtures booklet makes clear what this Dartmoor club feels about its ground. The cover shows a colour photograph of an idyllic scene of village cricket played in a sunlit glade surrounded by mature chestnuts, beeches, oaks and birches. On the far side, near the canvas sight screen, is a traditional low wooden pavilion, and unseen beyond the boundary, but well within six-hitting range, is the small, not always placid, river Wrey.

The club was formally constituted in 1938, although cricket has been played in the village since the 1880s. The ground belongs to the adjoining Wreyland Manor. A few owners back, the rent was raised substantially and the club received notice to quit. Fortunately, that owner moved on and subsequent purchasers regard having their own cricket team as a bonus and charge only a peppercorn rent.

More of an issue over the years has been a shortage of players. The club runs only one senior side which plays league cricket and friendlies on a Sunday. But it has a keen and growing junior section of boys and girls, begun in 2007, thanks to a grant from Access Sport. That doesn't entirely solve the problem as younger players don't always stay, but go on to play for other clubs when they move to senior school. The club has had very successful periods, particularly in the mid-90s when the three Wright brothers were in their prime. It won the Brockman Knockout Cup so regularly that Cup Officials reportedly tried to bar the club's best players from taking part.

Back in the days when the ground was cut by a horse-drawn mower, the outfield was so poor that few boundaries were scored. Once a motor mower was introduced, scores often reached 250 in 40-over games and more balls landed in the brook. To retrieve them, the club constructed a cage, which is charmingly featured on the club's badge, together with a bat and stumps. The ground is low-lying and once had a history of severe flooding. Cautiously, the club still does not schedule any home games in April.

Peter O'Toole, the actor, is remembered here with great affection. O'Toole was a long-time cricket lover and, when he had a son, qualified as a coach in order to teach him. He even founded his own club, The Lazarusians, and has an obituary in *Wisden*. He often brought his team to Lustleigh, which he called his 'favourite of all' cricket grounds. It was here that he played his last game. "The grounds are behind a church – they're beautiful, and there's a river," he said. "The thing to do at Lustleigh is to strike the ball into the river."

Club: Lustleigh C.C.

BELOW: Access to the ground is down a lane past the substantial base of an old Great Western Railway bridge.

BOTTOM: One of the most picturesque villages in Devon, Lustleigh has a gorgeous thatched tea room.

Lyndhurst

Hampshire

The playing area at Bolton's Bench in the New Forest is a quintessentially lovely English setting. Ponies add their own charm to the yew-surrounded ground, roaming around freely during matches. Like Bridgetown in Somerset, which is part-maintained by sheep, they graze the outfield helping to keep the grass in check, although a set of ancient and sturdy cast-iron rolling fences keeps them off the square.

A prominent hillock, or bench, overlooks the ground, where Lyndhurst and Ashurst have played since the early 1800s. It looks natural enough, but according to local legend the mount is actually the corpse of a dragon slain by Sir Maurice de Berkeley in the 1400s after a fierce battle which raged throughout the New Forest. Nothing to trouble *Time Team* here, then.

The first reports of cricket date back to 1816 when Lyndhurst played Lymington. The same two teams feature in a painting from 1846, which shows a good crowd watching from marquees and tents.

The land is owned by the Forestry Commission and the club pays an annual rent to compensate for loss of grazing. Any work on the outfield or pavilion has to be approved by that august body, the Verderers, who protect the New Forest from encroachment. Lyndhurst Cricket Club became one of the premier clubs in the New Forest and played league cricket for many years. During the 1950s and 60s it was a common sight to see cars parked all around the ground with many people coming to watch cricket of a high standard. In the 1980s, Lyndhurst joined forces with Deanery Cricket Club and became Lyndhurst and Deanery Cricket Club, but after initially flourishing the club stopped playing in the late 1990s and again in 2004.

The club was then taken over by a small local club (Ashurst) and became Lyndhurst and Ashurst. Since 2004, the club has steadily progressed and now plays in the Hampshire Cricket League, as well as Sunday friendlies and midweek evening league cricket. The club has also developed a successful colts section with U-9 and U-11 teams playing in the New Forest League.

The elegant thatched pavilion dates from 1888. Much time, effort and money has been spent improving its facilities over the last few years and it certainly doesn't show its age. "It has recently been re-thatched and is unrecognisable from what was inherited in 2004," says club chairman Andy Tuck, who is confident that this progress will continue.

Club: Lyndhurst & Ashurst C.C.

Valley of the Rocks, Lynton

Devon

With its sweeping views, dramatic rocks and changeable coastal weather, few grounds have the theatrical quality of the Valley of the Rocks. Lynton and Lynmouth have been fortunate enough to play their cricket here since 1876. They run just one side, with friendlies on Saturdays and league on Sundays, and seem to play for enjoyment as much as any burning desire to clamber out of the North Devon League, Division 3. Not long ago they were struggling to find players, but recently their ranks have been augmented by occasional weekenders from the city, keen on an afternoon's cricket. Mainly the team is made up of locals, such as Alex Spice, a player who has also taken on the role of groundsman.

According to club chairman, Robin May, Alex does a great job producing good cricket wickets without forgetting the environmental aspects. Spice, a builder, learned the job from scratch, following in the footsteps of his respected predecessor, the late Brian Hobbs. He works on his own, arriving on match day at 9.00 a.m.

"Problem is," he says, "if I'm not down to play, I sometimes find myself roped in if we're one short. Then it's a really long day!" Once a medium-pacer, Spice switched to leg-spin following injury, though he would still like to nip them off a length "because the wind here is usually 40 mph across the ground and the ball swings a mile." Batsmen also like playing here because the straight boundaries are only 40 yards off, though square of the wicket they can be 100 yards or so. The wind means that sightscreens are out of the question, a ready-made excuse for batsmen, one or two of whom, Spice admits, have taken a ball in the face.

This unique location has attracted teams from as far away as California and Australia in the last couple of seasons, and Robin May is frank that the 'green fee' is a great help in balancing the books.

The jewel of a pavilion, built of traditional stone, was burnt down by vandals in 1999, including most of the club's records and photos. But, cussedly, the club replaced it with an exact replica. Another feature of the area is a large herd of feral goats, which can appear high up in the rocks above the ground. They are not popular with locals because they eat the floral tributes in the cemetery amongst other things. A wire fence attempts to keep them off the square. Much more welcome are the local theatre companies which use the magnificent surroundings as a backdrop for productions of plays such as *Lorna Doone*, partly set in the Valley.

Club: Lynton & Lynmouth C.C.

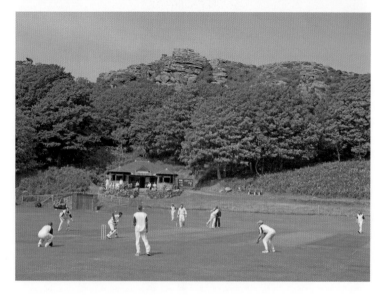

Marchwiel

Clwyd

It doesn't necessarily follow that a club with a beautiful home also has an outstanding cricket record. But Marchwiel & Wrexham – based at an elegant estate in the North Wales countryside and twice National Village Cup champions – qualifies on both counts with something to spare.

Founded in the 1920s, the club plays at Marchwiel Hall, a Grade II-listed Georgian-style country house with 150 acres of wooded grounds and glorious views over the Cheshire Plains. A cricket ground was first laid out in 1883 by owner Benjamin Piercy, and was considerably enhanced and extended by the builder Sir Robert McAlpine, just prior to the World War I.

Trees are a feature of this lovely setting, but the conker tree in front of the hall is a special landmark. It was here that The Conker Tree Stand was built for the McAlpine family to gather and watch the matches, especially during Cricket Week. Great players such as Sir Garfield Sobers and Sir Curtley Ambrose took part in this annual highlight which raised funds for charity.

Several of the McAlpines were talented cricketers. Sir Alfred played for Denbighshire in the late 1920s, completing an unusual double, as only a couple of years earlier he had been the county's High Sheriff. His son Jimmie also played for the county. Perhaps the most talented of the family cricketers was John Bell, Sir Alfred's grandson. A very effective leg-spinner and productive batsman, he was good enough to play for Wales on many occasions.

The picturesque pavilion with clock tower was built in 1920 and rebuilt and expanded in 1979. Inside are two plaques, one dedicated to the

memory of James Williams, a family member who died in the Somme offensive, and the other to John Bell's father, Peter, whose legacy funded the extension. Once a month a member of the club climbs into the attic area and gives the clock a good wind. Recent ground improvements include a replacement boundary fence courtesy of an ECB grant, and a new electronic scoreboard, thanks to a private donation from a local company.

Marchwiel & Wrexham run teams in the North Wales League, a Sunday team and three junior sides. The 1980s were undoubtedly its most successful period when the club twice went to Lord's and won the National Village Cup final. Celebrations included a tour of the village to show off the trophy. If the side is no longer quite the formidable outfit it once was, most clubs would be very satisfied with its lengthy honours board.

Club: Marchwiel & Wrexham C.C.

Menai Bridge

Anglesey

One day in the early 1970s, Eifion Jones was high up on a ladder repainting the exterior of a large country house in the small town of Menai Bridge on the Isle of Anglesey. From time to time, he stopped to admire the stunning panorama and the imposing Thomas Telford suspension bridge over the Menai Strait. His attention was also caught by a large nearby pasture in which a few sheep were idly grazing.

In his leisure hours, Eifion Jones was a founder member, and later president, of Menai Bridge Cricket Club. Formed in 1961, the club had led rather a nomadic existence over the years, playing at various different venues, such as Beaumaris Grammar School, the University ground in Bangor and even a farmer's field in Llanbedergoch. The team definitely needed a permanent home if it was going to develop.

When he came down from his ladder, Mr. Jones consulted his cricket club colleagues, along the lines of, 'Why's a nice field like that going to waste when it would make a perfectly good cricket ground for us?' The committee agreed

and enquiries were made. It turned out the field was the property of the County Council, but the council was open to the idea of developing it into a cricket facility.

In 1973, the club played its first match at its new home and since then Menai Bridge has thrived in the North Wales Premier Cricket League, winning two successive titles in 2014 and 2015. It runs four senior XIs, and a very active youth section which has developed many useful players for the senior sides. The stellar name is the former England and Glamorgan batsman, Matthew Maynard, whose late father Ken – a former Lancashire League player – also played for Menai Bridge.

By 2005, the club had made such progress that it was one of a relatively small number of clubs in England and Wales chosen by the ECB and Channel 4 to receive funding towards a new £150,000 pavilion. Current club president Keith Hughes, who's also responsible for groundcare, remembers that the club was given 12 months to raise £10,000 as proof of its commitment to the project. "It was very hard work but we made the deadline, thanks to our own fund-raising and a substantial much-appreciated grant from our landlord, Ynys Mon (Anglesey) County Council." On match days, Keith likes to look out over the picturesque view. "Do you know," he says, "we're the only cricket ground in Wales from which you can see Mount Snowdon?"

Club: Menai Bridge C.C.

Meopham

Kent

The origins of Meopham C.C. are lost in the mists of early Kent cricket history. The club modestly claims it was founded in about 1776, but a local inn changed its name to The Eleven Cricketers in 1735, so cricket must have been played on the Green before that. For a long time the pub – now called The Cricketers – was the club's headquarters and a constant source of refreshment during matches, providing kegs of beer which were wheeled across the Green. Links between pub and club grew ever stronger when, as happened from time to time, the landlords' family married cricketers.

The ground, overlooked by a magnificent six-sided windmill, is owned by the Parish Council and leased to the club for the enviably low annual rental of £1. Even the club agrees the Green is not the largest of playing areas. The ball is regularly hit out of the ground and the club doesn't dare play T20 to avoid collateral damage to cars. Fielders near the busy A227 have to take care as only a narrow ribbon of grass separates the boundary and the main road, though there is a low net to stop the ball mingling with traffic.

Back in the 1900s, when Meopham travelled to away games in the local undertaker's horse-drawn hearse, the ball had to cross the road and hit the kerb on the other side to count four. On one occasion, it continued rolling down the road and the batsmen ran 14 before it was returned. The opposite boundary is also a road and if the ball gets stuck in the long grass the batsmen have to run it out, although it is a four if you hit one of the boundary posts. Visiting captains should definitely brush up on the ground rules,

something a famous Meopham captain of the early 20th century, Major Robert Arnold, often failed to remind them about before the match commenced.

In its 250 years of existence, the club has been associated with many famous players. Valentine Romney, the outstanding Kent cricketer of his era, was born in Meopham in 1708, the son of the landlord of a local inn. In 1818, another local player, Thomas Nordish, became the only Meopham cricketer to play for England. The legendary Alfred Mynn also played here several times in the 1820s and 30s.

This was the era of Meopham's prime, according to William Gunyon's informative history written to celebrate the club's bicentenary in 1976, when several of the club's team played for Kent. Even so, Meopham were out for 11 in a game against West Peckham in 1835, its lowest-ever total. More recently, Peter May played here in 1949,

as did a teenage Alan Knott in 1961. In between, Sir Learie Constantine, remembered by the club with great affection, brought a team of West Indian Wanderers, attracting large crowds.

The club has moved on from employing a flock of geese to keep the grass down and using a small tent as a pavilion as it did in the 1890s. It competes very successfully in the Kent County Village League with teams in Divisions 1 and 4 and enjoys an annual Lads versus Dads game. Its current pavilion is a substantial wood construction complete with bar. Visitors can be sure of an excellent reception from Barbara Wade, the social secretary, and wife of former chairman Tony Wade. A local saying goes 'to be any good in Meopham you had to be good at cricket,' and they are in a long line of Meopham stalwarts devoted to keeping cricket alive at this historic ground.

Club: Meopham C.C.

RIGHT AND ABOVE: Protective measure are in place to prevent lusty blows breaking groundfloor windows in the row of cottages at the top end of the ground. There are also ample signs in place warning of the likely impact of a cricket ball on cars parked just off the green in front of them.

Mountnessing

Essex

In 1991, Highwood Hospital C.C. in Brentwood folded after its ground was sold off for a housing development. Wondering where their cricket was going to come from the following season, three of the team, Alan Barnby, John Ellis and Dave Mitchell, met over a pint in the Prince of Wales pub in the nearby village of Mountnessing. Though small, Mountnessing had a large recreation area, the Coronation Field, where tennis and football were played. The trio decided to ask the Parish Council if it could be used for cricket as well. Cricket in the village went back to about 1920 but had been played in a farmer's field and died out before World War II.

With the council quick to give the go-ahead, the club was reformed and began to play in 1992, but only away games. Meanwhile, a new square with nine pitches was prepared by the same trio and a new pavilion built. It wasn't till May 1993 that the first home game took place against the nearby small town of Hutton with England and Essex fast bowler Neil Foster officially opening the ground.

To outsiders, the park is virtually begging to be a cricket venue. It is an impressive, almost manicured 5-acre expanse encircled by beautiful mature trees. But the park's 'jewel in the crown', to quote former captain and club chairman Alan Barnby, is the Mountnessing Windmill. Windmills are a rarity these days and it is rarer still to find a working model at a ground. A Grade II-listed post mill, it dates back to 1807, though there are records of a windmill on the site in 1477. Now owned by the Parish Council, it has been restored to full working order thanks to much hard work by the Friends organisation, and attracts many visitors. According to Alan Barnby, the windmill also tempts visiting batsmen. "Coronation Field is relatively small," he says, "and the Mill looks like an easy target." But, he goes on, "most batsmen have lost their bet over the years and the mill has been struck on very few occasions."

The club played in the Mid-Essex League for 20 years, but had difficulty attracting new players and withdrew in 2016. Though it still plays a Sunday side, its Saturday team has now amalgamated with old rivals, Hutton, and provides about half the side. Hutton uses Mountnessing as its second ground for Fifth team, colts and ladies fixtures. With its new modernised pavilion, Mountnessing is confident that cricket at the ground has a future. It's a great place to be a spectator and if you time your visit right, there is free entry to the windmill.

Clubs: Mountnessing C.C., Hutton C.C.

Mytholmroyd

Yorkshire

The outskirts of the village of Mytholmroyd is one of the most beautiful areas of countryside in the Upper Calder Valley. A rich variety of trees stretch as far as the eye can see up both sides of the valley. Founded in 1894, the club has always made its home in these lovely surroundings and, thanks to the ground's former owner, the late Victor Ingham, can play here rent-free for as long as it exists.

Mytholmroyd joined what is now the South West Halifax League in 1914, but it was not until 1948 that the club became Division 1 champions for the first time. Their success was founded on excellent performances by ace bowlers, Charlie Pugh and Bert Wilcock. In one of those oddities beloved of cricket statisticians, the two bowlers took the same number of wickets (71) for the same number of runs (475), naturally giving them identical bowling average (6.69). Usually comfortably placed in the Premier Division First XI League, Mytholmroyd most recently won the title in 2007, doing the double by also winning the prestigious knock-out format Parish Cup.

Mytholmroyd runs two senior Saturday sides and a Sunday team, but junior sides have been temporarily suspended. Facilities and equipment are as state-of-the-art as the budget will allow. The club is particularly proud of its new double

sightscreens on adjustable rails, which are the best in the league, according to club elder Nigel Robinson. Finances are much helped by income from letting the pavilion. With a dance floor and bar, it is a popular social centre for the village.

Mytholmroyd's name derives from the Old English for 'a settlement where two rivers meet' and it is an unfortunate fact that the area is very prone to flooding. In June 2000, the club was preparing for the official opening of its new pavilion, largely funded by Sport England and the National Lottery. Celebrations included a match between the club and a representative XI. Overnight a tremendous storm broke, flooding the field and making any official activities out of the question. More recently, the devastating 2015 floods left the pitch under water and covered with silt. Fortunately the ECB and YCB invested money to help with the clear-up operation. The good news is that a new flood management plan, including the planting of thousands of trees, will begin to make an impact in the not-too-distant future.

Club: Mytholmroyd C.C.

Nettlebed

Oxfordshire

The Rec, where Nettlebed C.C. plays, lies back from the Oxfordshire village's main road, almost as if it doesn't want to be found. Glance up as you're driving past and you can just glimpse it at the top of a lane. It is a very pleasant ground in a dell enclosed by trees. Haig whisky liked it so much that in 1977 they took a publicity shot of the ground and the Nettlebed team, which appeared in advertisements all over the country. In the mid-sixties, a *Look at Life* film on village cricket also featured the Rec with the club president, the writer and explorer Peter Fleming, riding up to the pavilion on his horse.

According to the writer Duff Hart-Davis's history of the club, back in the 1900s it was 'a derelict area of humps and hollows known as "The Puddles" from which sand and clay had been dug to make bricks since the 14th century.' Peter Fleming's grandfather, the banker Robert Fleming, converted the land into a recreation area in 1908. The club, founded in about 1870, was then playing in the grounds of nearby Joyce Grove where Peter Fleming and his younger brother Ian, creator of James Bond, lived as children. As a quid pro quo for planning permission to extend the house and gardens, Fleming was required to develop the Common for community use.

Work was completed in 1909, but by laying out the ground perfectly level and using brushwood, the builders created a serious drainage problem that still plagues the club today. The budget about that time was £16, Hart-Davis says, which included the purchase of one set of stumps 'with revolving tops' and two 'single, right-handed batting gloves for right-handed batsmen.' Opponents were often servants' teams from Oxford colleges. The club secretary was paid 10% of the subscriptions and membership quickly rose.

The original rather rudimentary pavilion dating to 1910 – one changing room and no running water – was eventually modernised in the 1950s. It couldn't be more welcoming today with a bar and kitchen where sumptuous teas are prepared by Jodie Butler, wife of the club captain, Michael Butler. The square is in good shape with nine pitches, but the club admits the outfield is a bit uneven, blaming the old clay pit and original brushwood which has gradually sunk.

The club runs one team and plays only friendlies. Every year there is a game against an XI raised by the current president, a grandson of the original Peter Fleming and also named Peter. A ground-sharing arrangement with nearby Henley C.C., whose Third and Fourth XIs play here, means the Rec is well-used and brings in welcome funds. The club has not been short of famous cricketing visitors including Percy Fender and Jim Laker. If Laker is renowned for taking all 10 wickets on two occasions, the club can point to its own Jim – Jim Hutton, who took 10 for 10 in 1950.

Clubs: Nettlebed C.C.

North Nibley

Gloucestershire

When North Nibley relocated in 1999, the club moved to a Gloucestershire paradise. At one end of the ground, the backdrop of a sweeping landscape and Stinchcombe Hill; at the other, Nibley House, a Grade II-listed Georgian manor house.

The club was formed in 1994 and up till 1999 rented a ground used by another team. Then a local landowner, the late David Stokes, gifted the village around three acres of land. Jubilee Field was just large enough for a full-size football pitch and a cricket ground, allowing for some overlap. Stokes arranged for the field to be levelled and reseeded and the square was professionally laid. The ground is a valuable village resource, which the local primary school uses as an overflow playground and for sport, including cricket coaching. Some of the current team got their start in this way.

Initially, the club didn't have a pavilion and used the billiard room in Nibley House as a tea room. With Lottery funding unavailable, finance was finally raised for a well-equipped pavilion, thanks to the generosity of local benefactors and the community. On display is the club's prize possession – a Freddie Flintoff bat autographed by the great man, 'Good luck with the pavilion'.

North Nibley runs just the one senior XI which plays local friendlies on Sundays and T20 games on Wednesday evenings in the small but highly competitive Pratt Cup. The club seems in excellent shape with membership growing and the average age of the players reducing. An annual highlight is the vice-presidents' game, a 40-overs-a-side match at which the club's benefactors are invited to enjoy a sumptuous tea washed down with plenty of Pimm's. The club's teas are, in its own words, "spectacular", thanks to the tea ladies organised by Wynne Holcombe, who doubles as club scorer.

As the club doesn't run a bar, it has to be inventive in its search for income. One year it decided to play a dawn-to-dusk match on Midsummer Day. The game got off to a promising start at 4:00 a.m., but by 9:00 a.m. everyone had disappeared. The experiment wasn't repeated. A more reliable source of income is the North Nibley music festival, a very popular weekend event which raises money for good causes, some of which filters through to help maintain Jubilee Field.

Club: North Nibley C.C.

Northop Hall

Flintshire

According to a past chairman and former captain, Northop is like one of those football teams which struggle at the foot of the Premiership – too small to challenge the bigger clubs, but always up for a scrap.

While it's true that the village plays against larger towns like Bangor and mighty Llandudno, nothing suggests that the club's organisation or ambitions are small scale. Its support and facilities are superb and the immaculately cared-for ground in the shadow of the 6th century St. Eurgain's Church is as beautiful as you could wish. The church's ancient stone wall is also the boundary and hitting the ball into the churchyard raises a big cheer.

Northop was founded in 1864, the same year that *Wisden* was first published, overarm bowling was legalised, and W. G. Grace scored his first century in a major match. Like many teams of the period, Northop played under the auspices of the local gentry, in this case the Bankes family of Soughton Hall. One of the family – subsequently Lord Justice Bankes – was captain of the team in 1871. In the 1890s, he generously offered Northop use of the Flint Road field, where it still plays.

The club competes in the North Wales Cricket League and was promoted to the First XI Premier Division in 2017 after winning Division 1. The

Second XI also won its league. Northop runs three senior elevens, five junior sides and a girls' team. Several of the younger players have won regional recognition and some have achieved full national honours for Wales. Successful women cricketers include Rachel Warrender, who played for the Wales Women's team, which would have pleased St. Eurgain, daughter of Caractacus and reputedly Christianity's first female saint.

But most fun seems to be had by the Irregulars, described in the club newsletter as 'a motley crew of hypochondriacs and retired cricketers who haven't picked up a bat since leaving school.' The club celebrates each new cricket season with a massive turnout of volunteers to spring-clean the ground and pavilion and there are plenty of projects to raise funds for charity and the club.

To celebrate its 150th anniversary in 2014, the club published a very enjoyable volume of reminiscences. It is well worth reading to discover how, in 1979, Ifor Roberts ended up fielding at square leg for Overton at Overton, when he thought he was playing for Northop at Marchwiel and how nine-man Northop still managed to win.

Club: Northop C.C.

Old Town

Yorkshire

Old Town C.C. close to Hebden Bridge in West Yorkshire has moved not once, but twice, since it was formed in 1885. Boston Hill Cricket ground – surrounded by oaks, silver birches and sycamores and in a lovely setting at the foot of Wadsworth Moor near the Calder Valley – is its current and, no doubt, final home.

Old Town's first ground was at Middle Nook Farm on the edge of the moor, described as 'bleak and isolated'. After suffering some heavy beatings, the club disbanded in 1891 but reorganised three years later, moving to Old Laithe in the Chisley area in 1895. Its playing standards had vastly improved by the time it left the ground in 1957. It had won the Hebden Bridge League and other competitions several times and never been out of the top two in the League for the whole of the post-World War II decade.

But gradually, it became clear that the facilities and location at Old Laithe didn't meet the standards of the day. The ground was small and uneven and lacked services such as water, which had to be brought to the ground for each match. After a search lasting several years, the club bought its current 3¼-acre field in 1954. Clearing the ground of obstructions such as 130 trees and a large circular tank took three years. The National Playing Fields and the West Riding Playing Fields Associations contributed much appreciated grants to meet some of the £2,000 cost. The balance was raised by the club itself, its players and supporters. The heavy roller arrived, hauled through the village by a group of particularly dedicated members. The same team also built the wooden pavilion, which was significantly upgraded in 1997, thanks to funding from the Sports Council and Calderdale Council.

Old Town's two teams currently play in the Halifax Cricket League. The First team, under their captain Adil Shah, usually sits comfortably in mid-table of Division 2. The Seconds however finished bottom in 2017. They avoided relegation only because there wasn't a league below them. Local photographer Ross McGinnes showed just how important a part a cricket club and its pavilion can play in the local community when he chronicled a year in the life of Old Town. The month-by-month gallery showed its use for playgroups to folk clubs and fireworks parties, with a little bit of cricket thrown in.

Club: Old Town C.C.

RIGHT: Old Town First XI batting against Outlane C.C. in a Halifax Cricket League fixture in the scenic ground above Hebden Bridge.

Oxted

Surrey

Oxted lies at the foot of the North Downs in Surrey. The cricket club dates to around 1890 following the 1884 arrival of the railway line allowing direct commuter access to London and increasing the populations of both Oxted and neighbouring Limpsfield.

Given the remarkable list of teams playing at Oxted and Limpsfield Cricket Club, it's surprising that the two teams needed to merge, but merge they did in 2006 to create a behemoth of a village cricket set-up. Oxted brought their Master Park pavilion and ground to the relationship, Limpsfield contributed their pavilion and ground at Grub Street, and just to make matters even more complicated for a beleaguered fixtures secretary, they added the nearby Crockham Hill ground.

But when you have a First, Second, Third, Fourth and Fifth team; a Saturday Friendly XI, a Sunday XI (presumably less friendly), a Crockham Hill XI, and Under-18, Under-19 and Under-21 teams, not forgetting the Surrey Slam T20 XI and a Ladies XI, that's a lot of senior cricket to schedule. Plus there are ten junior sides, two minis and a girls' side.

At Master Park, long-standing fixtures included one against Gaieties C.C., the cricket club founded in 1937 by music hall artist Lupino Lane, whose company was at that time based at the Gaiety Theatre. From 1972 the club was captained by playwright Harold Pinter and the club treasures an irate letter sent to them by

Pinter after Oxted cancelled their game at the very last minute.

From the 1930s until the 1970s Oxted were supported by Surrey CCC who sent a number of sides containing their top players. Tony Lock, who played for England in the 1950s, was a local boy, born in Limpsfield. On one occasion, in a benefit match set up for Ken Barrington, Gary Sobers batted for Oxted and amongst his mighty blows were damage to the roof of a spectator's car (which Sobers duly signed) and a lofted drive across the road into the garden of the British Legion.

Oxted are hoping to renew and enlarge their pavilion so it can be used as a community sports resource, along with buying a new set of covers for a large square which boasts sixteen pitches. One of their 2012 fund-raising schemes was to hold a beer festival at the cricket club, which proved so enormously successful (who could have seen that happening at a cricket club) that it has become an annual three-day event. Showcasing over 100 real ales, over 10,000 visitors are expected for the 2018 festival, for which the beer doesn't stop play.

Club: Oxted and Limpsfield C.C.

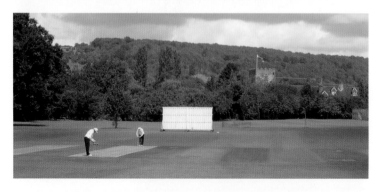

RIGHT: Despite possessing two Bowdryers, Oxted and Limpsfield only have sheeting for covers at Master Park. Thus, when a summer shower interrupts play, it's a scene very much like putting the covers on at Wimbledon.

Patterdale

Cumbria

'The prettiest field in England' declared William Wordsworth of the Ullswater Way where Patterdale C.C. plays cricket. He had been taking one of his famous creative walks through what is now called the King George V Playing Fields. It's a shame that was a hundred or so years before regular cricket started here, otherwise he might have composed a few lines on a Patterdale match. Which isn't as unlikely as it might seem: an 1802 sonnet contains the lines '...those boys who in yon meadow ground/In white-sleev'd shirts are playing by the score...'

The ground is set in a beautiful park bordered by a wonderful variety of trees including sycamores, oaks, holly, ash and Douglas firs, and is overlooked by many majestic Lakeland fells such as Place Fell, Boredale Hause and Helvellyn, the third highest peak in England. A Victorian

church, built from local stone and once part of the estate, sits just beyond the boundary. The spectacular setting earned the ground second place in the *Daily Telegraph*'s 2013 Willow Walks competition.

That said, you can't have everything. The weather can be famously changeable and in 2015 the ground felt the effect of Storm Desmond which overflowed the nearby Grisedale Beck and flooded the outfield. The area has one of the busiest mountain rescue services in the country and helicopters regularly touch down, though they avoid the square and its six pitches.

The club was formed in 1923 and for a good number of years played only friendlies. In 1960 it joined the Eden Valley League where it continues to play, memorably winning all

six competitions it entered in 1976. The team is drawn almost entirely from locals; farmers, firemen, builders and plumbers (though the firemen are sometimes called away for more important duties in the middle of a game) and also features the chairman of the local Parish Council, Rob Shephard. Like many other clubs, it suffers from a lack of younger players which has caused it to withdraw from the Wednesday Night Village League.

The Pavilion, shared with the local football club, dates back to the 1930s. Despite many additions and improvements over the years by volunteers, it is showing its age and funds are being raised for a new one. The club received a grant for a Mobile Wicket Cover via a Waitrose-supported ECB Scheme in 2015, but is heavily reliant on volunteers for ground maintenance under the leadership of Richard Kelso, the club chairman.

A highlight in the club's history was the visit by the Lord's Taverners in June 2002 to support the area after the disastrous 2001 Foot and Mouth epidemic. The visiting side included former England players Brian Close, Fred Rumsey, Graham Roope and Peter Lever, and actors Robert Powell and John Alderton. When the forthright Brian Close was out, he complained it was the worst ball he'd ever received and blamed it on the poor condition of the wicket. 'Be told!' as they say in northern parts, and the club promptly dug up and relaid three of the pitches.

Club: Patterdale C.C.

Penshurst Place

Kent

At Penshurst Place, both the estate and the cricket club have historical associations to spare. The magnificent medieval house was built in the 14th century and its owners have included princes, dukes and two kings. Henry VIII became owner after beheading the Duke of Buckinghamshire – the property of a 'traitor' conveniently reverted to the Crown. Edward VI gifted the castle to his tutor, Sir William Sydney, and descendants of the family still own the Grade-I listed building today.

The cricket lineage is distinguished in its own right and can be traced back to the birth of organised cricket with a game recorded at Penshurst as early as 1724. The current club was formed in 1752 and proudly calls itself 'the oldest privately-owned club in England'. It is easy to take a couple of wrong turns into various parts of the grounds before finding the driveway to the cricket pitch. Once there, however, visiting sides love the stunning view of the main building. The boundary fence can be a hazard to a fielder chasing a cover drive and batsmen have to clear the fence to earn a maximum. Hitting it on the full earns only four.

The club was a founder member of the Kent County Village League in 1990 and has played in the top division of the Kent County Village League without break since 1996 with a dramatic purple patch from 2012-14 when it won a hat-trick of titles. It runs two Saturday sides, a Sunday team and a Friendly XI. A junior side is in abeyance following the sad death of the coach, Ken Watters.

Club: Penshurst Park C.C.

Raby Castle

Staindrop, County Durham

There can be few, if any, more perfect images of a certain type of English village cricket than a beautiful venue overlooked by the historic ramparts of a castle. Raby Castle C.C. has played in such magnificent surroundings since 1890, although the ground was the site of the first officially recorded game of cricket in County Durham as long ago as 1751.

While the cricketing experience could easily be overwhelmed by its setting, it isn't here. The ground is immaculate with a close-mown outfield and well-prepared pitch, thanks to a lot of hard work by volunteers. One group works on the outfield and fencing twice a week and another looks after the pitch. Players are unlikely to find many better tended grounds and to the non-expert, there's no reason why the ground couldn't host higher level matches. The club gives off a nice atmosphere of good old-fashioned keenness on the field and off and enjoyed an exceptional season in 2017, winning no less than four trophies.

The square is surprisingly big with twelve pitches. Batsmen who favour swinging across the line will hope to play on the wicket nearest the castle, where a six is not much more than a gentle hoick over the fence. Deer, which freely roam the park, equally find no difficulty in clearing the fence onto the outfield but quickly make the reverse leap if approached.

The club appreciates its excellent relations with the castle owner, Lord Barnard, and his staff. The immaculately-kept gardens, as well as the castle itself, are well worth exploring if you want to wander away from the cricket for a while. If the dining room and terrace seem familiar, they were featured in ITV's drama series *Victoria*.

It is hard to believe that playing here has any downsides but, following gales at the start of 2017, some of the beautiful trees in the outfield may have to be felled for safety reasons. And while the club fields teams in the Darlington & District Cricket League, it has concerns about the future. The club has run a junior set-up in the past, but currently there isn't the interest in the U-13 and U-15 age groups. The club is also conscious that the 1980 pavilion could do with an extension if only to accommodate the larger cricket bags now in vogue.

Club: Raby Castle C.C.

Ramsbottom

Lancashire

Ramsbottom is a village on the river Irwell between Bury and Blackburn in Lancashire. It's in the heart of mill country and first started playing games in 1845 before moving to its Acre Bottom site in 1864. Even before the start of the Lancashire Leagues the club employed a professional, the first being Arthur Thornton from Saltaire who was paid (an almost Ben Stokes-like) £54 for the 1881 season.

In October 1890 the club joined the North East Lancashire Cricket League. The forerunner of the Lancashire League, clubs affiliated were Accrington, Bacup, Burnley, Church, Colne, East Lancashire, Enfield, Haslingden, Lowerhouse, Nelson, Ramsbottom, Rawtenstall and Todmorden, with the addition of Rishton a month later. It's been much the same ever since.

In June 2002 Ramsbottom posted their highest total to date at Acre Bottom, an unassailable 307-4. Todmodern in reply were bowled out for a paltry 115. Star of the show that day was their professional, a young Aussie batsman called Michael Clarke who scored 178. Whatever happened to him…?

Another standout moment came in June 2009 when fourteen-year-old Tom Parton became the youngest player to make his First XI League debut versus Bacup at the tender age of 14 years and 113 days.

While Oxted and Limpsfield Cricket Club host a beer festival to raise money for local sporting charities, Ramsbottom has started up its own music festival. The three-day music fest held at Acre Bottom in the middle of September – importantly, after the last game has been played – has a varied line-up, with international acts mixed with up-and-coming new talent. The Stranglers and Beth Orton topped the bill in 2017 while in 2018 the Boomtown Rats are scheduled to headline on Sunday night. It started off life as the Ramsbottom Musical Festival, but presumably that sounded a little too 'folky' and now it's known as Head For The Hills.

Club: Ramsbottom C.C.

BELOW: Action at Acre Bottom as Ramsbottom C.C. Second XI take on East Lancs C.C. Second XI.

Rawtenstall

Lancashire

Formed in 1885, Rawtenstall is one of the elite group of sides that make up the Lancashire League. Nicknamed 'Rocky' the club plays at The Worswick Memorial Ground in the centre of a village at the edge of the Pennines, sitting alongside Rossendale, Haslingden and New Hall Hey. The ground, a gift of the Worswick family in 1955, is large and impressive. A large, recently refurbished 19th-century cotton mill is a dominating presence in the background.

A founder member of the League, Rawtenstall has won the title on seven occasions, most recently in 1982, and the Worsley Cup knockout tournament, four times. Before and after World War II, Lancashire League grounds were the only places in Britain to see some of the greatest names ever to have played the game. League rules permitted each club to play one professional, often an overseas star. Among Rawtenstall's pros, older cricket lovers will recall Vijay Hazare, the Indian Test captain, and George Tribe, a wonderful Australian all-rounder barely recognised by the selectors. More recently, Australian Test player Michael Bevan and West Indian Franklyn Stephenson played for the club. According to Michael Atherton, the stars were expected to bowl through an innings unchanged and to score the majority of the runs. Pre-war, Sydney Barnes was reportedly taken to task by the Rawtenstall committee after one game for not getting seven wickets in a match: "Pro, what exactly are we paying you for?"

Visiting teams brought the likes of Sir Learie Constantine, Sir Viv Richards, Sir Wes Hall, Basil D'Oliviera, Michael Holding and Allan Donald to the ground. Small wonder that the black-and-white photos of the 1950s show spectators squeezed into every available seat on the famous terraces in front of the pavilion. League professionals are not so high profile these days, although Rawtenstall's pro for 2018 was KP – no, not that one, but the South African all-rounder, Keegan Petersen.

The club went through a difficult period a decade or so ago when it lacked funds to replace the ageing clubhouse which was uninsurable because of deterioration. Fortunately the issue was resolved and the present impressive two-storey pavilion building was opened in 2009. Unlike traditional village cricket matches, teams don't socialise during the tea interval but eat their sandwiches separately in their dressing room, no doubt hatching plans for the next session. The club runs three senior XIs, a T20 side on Friday evenings and four junior sides. While there is no women's team, Emma Pickup, an effective medium-pacer, was captain of the Second XI in 2017.

Club: Rawtenstall C.C.

Saltaire

Yorkshire

Saltaire C.C. in Roberts Park preserves a pleasing period atmosphere and, as part of a UNESCO World Heritage site since 2001, will probably never change significantly.

Built from scratch beside the River Aire in the mid-19th century, Saltaire village was the brainchild of Sir Titus Salt. Salt, who manufactured worsted cloth using alpaca wool, wanted to move his workers away from the appalling pollution of nearby Bradford. The new village came complete with a famous innovative mill, housing, hospital, church and railway station – everything, in fact, except a pub, as Salt was a supporter of the temperance movement.

Construction work began in 1851 and took 25 years to complete with the 5-acre cricket ground opening in 1871. Roberts Park is the only permanent cricket ground situated in a World Heritage site (although competitive cricket is also played at Spianada Square in Corfu Town). The ground had a narrow escape in the early eighties, when a trunk road was planned which would have bisected the park and brought an end to the cricket. Thanks to a protest led by a group of local sports clubs, in which the Saltaire player Pat McKelvey was influential, the proposal was shelved.

Although bordered by many buildings, the ground retains a pastoral feel and has many fans, including Sir Learie Constantine, the West Indian cricketer and politician. 'Some of the loveliest grounds I have played on are Perth in Western Australia, Todmorden (Lancashire League) and Saltaire,' he recorded in his autobiography.

Among the outstanding cricketers who have played for the club, most notable is the great England bowler Sydney Barnes. From 1915 to 1923, the 40-plus Barnes took 904 wickets at only 5.26 and Saltaire won the Bradford Cricket League championship three times. In 1938, another famous name made his debut. England off-spinner Jim Laker, now honoured by a plaque on the side of the club's scoreboard, was brought up in Saltaire and was reckoned more of a batsman than a bowler.

Saltaire now plays in the Airedale & Wharfedale Senior Cricket League and runs two senior and three junior sides. In recent years, it was badly hit by the Boxing Day Flood of 2015 which left the ground, pavilion, scorebox and Half Moon Café under 4 feet of water.

Funds for the club come from running the permanent Saltaire Cricket Club Table Top in Victoria Hall and the recently-reopened Half Moon Café. The statue of Sir Titus on its roof surprisingly faces away from the cricket. He would no doubt be pleased that the village of Saltaire remains much as originally planned, and also with the bronze statues of two alpacas in front of the cafe, but less so that alcohol can be obtained at a local restaurant called Don't Tell Titus.

Club: Saltaire C.C.

ABOVE: With a ground adjacent to the river Aire, Saltaire can anticipate floods during the winter months. Likewise, being located in the north of England, it can also expect snow.

Sedgwick

Cumbria

The three indispensable features of a traditional English village are generally reckoned to be a church, a pub and a village green where the local club can play cricket.

With no pub, no church, no village green and no shops either, the charming Cumbrian village of Sedgwick doesn't fit the usual template. The village's centrepiece is Sedgwick House, a listed 19th-century country house built for a gunpowder manufacturer, William Wakefield. When the family moved out pre-World War II, the building became a school and is now a residential block of apartments.

The glory of the house is its spacious grounds and many fine specimen trees. Both William Wakefield and his son Jacob were keen cricketers and laid out a ground in a meadow adjacent to the house. They formed an estate side and played against nomadic sides, one of whom included none other than W. G. Grace, whose letter hangs proudly in the pavilion.

Formed in 1947, the club's first home was in nearby Levens, but in 1950 it was invited to use the Sedgwick House ground by Lancashire County Council. The club now owns the ground bought from the developer of the apartments for a nominal sum.

In 1971, lack of players forced Sedgwick to fold, but it reformed six years later after a friendly between two local pubs showed there was enough local enthusiasm to support a team. Starting off in Division 5 of the Westmorland Cricket League, by 1990 Sedgwick had reached Division 1, and has now won three championship titles. It currently runs two adult teams and three junior sides. Weather is changeable in these parts and in 2017 the club lost so many games to rain that it was relegated.

Among Sedgwick's treasured memories are Graeme Fowler scoring over 200 in a benefit game and the visit of Test umpire John Holder. "He stayed behind after the game, chatting to everyone," says Robin Willacy, doyen of the club and head of the prominent Willacy clan. No doubt Holder enjoyed a drop of something in the pavilion, a delightful construction in the old-fashioned style with wooden balcony and criss-cross beams. The club would love to extend it and approached the ECB for a grant. "But they want it to be more modern," says club chairman Phil Evans, "and we love it the way it is. At the end of a game, we sit here with a glass in our hand and watch the sun going down over the Lyth valley. No-one rushes home."

Club: Sedgwick C.C.

Sheepscombe

Gloucestershire

Laurie Lee Field, where Sheepscombe C.C. play, is a beautiful, idiosyncratic ground with inspiring views of the Cotswolds hills and valleys. The famous poet, born and bred in the area, owned it from 1971 till his death in 1997, although the club has played there since 1896. Lee, who lived in the neighbouring village of Slad, allowed the club to play rent-free and the ground was named after him as a thank-you. His uncles were founder members and strong links with the famous writer remain.

Another resonant local name is the poet Frank Mansell, a friend of Laurie Lee. Lee is the better known writer, but in Sheepscombe they still talk of the time Mansell – a slippery seamer, according to reports – took 10 for 8 in an innings in 1961. For some years, the Mansell Trophy was awarded to the club's most successful bowler.

When the playing field's future came into question in 2014, the club could have been forced out of existence. Through an energetic and original fund-raising campaign called 'Stump Up', £25,000 was raised in only six months. Aided by an equal contribution from the ECB, the ground was purchased and the future of cricket at Sheepscombe assured. Enough funds remained to upgrade the clubhouse facilities and expand the coaching programme.

The club runs a First team on Saturdays and plays with plenty of enthusiasm and skill in the Gloucester County Cricket League. A Friendly XI plays on Sundays and it also runs an U-13 and U-11s for boys and girls. The club welcomes new players of all ages, says club Chairman Elisabeth Skinner, who stresses the value of the club in keeping the young men attached to the village where they grew up or went to primary school. "In a village like Sheepscombe where property is expensive, young people find it difficult to buy – the cricket club allows them to come back if they've moved to Stroud."

No-one would say that Laurie Lee Field is the most accessible of grounds, but getting there is definitely worth the effort. Walkers can take a very steep path up from the village pub, the picturesque Butcher's Arms, recommended only to those with healthy hearts and unencumbered by cricket bags. The easier route is by car, although it is single track and mainly unpaved. Eventually you reach the heath and park near the pavilion, passing an unusual stone memorial bench to a former player, Steve Proctor.

Standing on the pavilion verandah, a first reaction is to wonder what has happened to the boundary on the far side. The ground slopes away very rapidly, dropping as much as 15 feet (4.6 metres). Long leg can see only the top half of a batsman and needs to be alerted if a ball is coming downhill in his direction, although if it is, the chances are its momentum will beat him anyway. Although Frank Mansell reportedly chose to bowl from that end, the average fast bowler probably would not, though it might give him an added element of surprise as he appears out of nowhere up the hill.

Club: Sheepscombe C.C.

LEFT: Even viewed from a raised pavilion, the drop-off beyond the square is evident.

ABOVE: Sheepscombe's Ollie Bruce is the fifth successive generation of his family (mostly bowlers) to play for the side, the first being Albert Hopkins a local farmer. Ollie ploughs his furrow in the world of media.

Shobrooke Park

Crediton, Devon

Shobrooke Park C.C. are a club in the great tradition of English cricket teams, playing in the grounds of a grand country estate. Entry to the ground is via the South Lodge (not the North Lodge or the East Lodge), yet unlike so many other venues in this book, there is no large stately pile.

A deer park is said to have existed at Shobrooke since the early 16th century. Richard Hippisley Tuckfield inherited the estate in 1807, and commissioned Henry Hakewill to build a house, known as Little Fulford, on a site within the old deer park. With the demise of grand country estates following World War I, by the time of the second, the renamed Shobrooke Park Mansion was being used to accommodate St Peter's Court Preparatory School, which had been evacuated from Broadstairs just after war broke out.

A ruinous fire in 1945 killed three boys and destroyed the house, however the landscaped parkland and lake remain much as the 19th-century landscape architects intended. The cricket club have two soaring cedar trees at the lake end of the ground, but it is a dead tree at the South Lodge end that commands the most attention.

When the canopy of a Scots pine at the boundary's edge was felled by a winter gale, its immediate destination appeared to be the log pile. But cricketers Steve Jones, a tree surgeon, and his friend Bruce Kerry, a keen woodworker,

set about carving the remaining stump into a unique feature in village cricket (a kind of Claes Oldenburg-tribute for the West Country). After eighteen months of work, and using an old Duncan Fearnley bat as their 'artist's model', the 1890 pine was ready for its reveal sponsored by local estate agents Helmores, who awarded a prize for the first cricketer to hit it.

The wooden obelisk stands 16 feet high (4.8 metres), the blade is 2 feet wide and it took 360 feet (110 metres) of polypropylene rope to bind the handle. Despite its failure to meet the dimensions set by the MCC for cricket bats, and also the small fact that it is still attached to the ground, the giant bat may yet make it to the middle.

The plan is to cut the bat free from the stump when the base eventually starts to rot and lean it up against some of the other magnificent trees around the ground.

Shobrooke Park run two teams in the Devon Cricket League, the First XI in the B Division and the Second XI which currently sit in Corinthian Pool 2.

Club: Shobrooke Park C.C.

Sicklinghall

North Yorkshire

Sicklinghall is a small village of about 300 near the market town of Wetherby in North Yorkshire, with a local club which has gone through some extraordinary times since 2016. Its current home, Kirkby Lane, on the edge of the village where the fields begin to stretch away, is its fourth ground. The club last relocated in 2002 when it moved from Stockeld Park – the 'big house' in the area – to make way for a Christmas Adventure Park.

Sicklinghall, like most clubs, has had its ups and downs, such as occasional relegations, but nothing had prepared it for the events of the night of 8th October 2016 when four vandals reduced the clubhouse, scorebox, toilets and equipment store to a charred wreck.

Although arson or other attacks on cricket clubs are not uncommon, the club was sent reeling by the shock. However, under the strong leadership of its then chairman, Andy Wood, and his successor, Zai Ali, it has made a remarkable comeback.

Fortunately, Ali, a former club captain, has a background in the house building industry and in accountancy, giving him ideal experience for coping with the situation. He is the first to pay tribute to the various organisations, both local and national, who rallied round.

The Parish Council made an immediate grant towards the cost of temporary buildings for the 2017 season; the Yorkshire Cricket Board (YCB) was in touch the very next day, offering £500 and has continued to be very supportive. With the help of a grant from the ECB's emergency fund, Sicklinghall rented two Portakabins for the 2017 season at a cost of £7,500. "Realistically," says

Ali, "it will be at least 2019 before further ECB funding is decided, there's a very long queue."

On the field, the club runs one senior XI and, with an eye on the future, an U-9 side. It has learned to love its two Portakabins and had an inspiring season in 2017, finishing third in the league. It gave up the chance to finish second by reversing the batting order for the last game. Unfortunately, the club's painful experiences have a sting in the tail. Almost the first replacement equipment the club bought was a ride-on mower. Within two weeks it had been stolen.

Club: Sicklinghall C.C.

Sidmouth

Devon

According to the official blue plaque on the Sidmouth pavilion, 'Cricket was first played here in 1823 and the first "Cricket House" erected in 1827,' which means that Sidmouth C.C. will soon be celebrating its bicentenary.

The club has many other reasons to feel proud. It plays at a magnificent location overlooking Lyme Bay and has an outstanding record of local cricket success over many years. The plaque goes on to say – surprisingly considering the Somerset border is 20 miles off – that Sidmouth was the birthplace of Somerset CCC in 1875, a decision taken after a game against the Gentlemen of Devon.

The links between club and county have been long and enduring with players moving from club to county and back. Currently, the highly promising off-spinner Dom Bess, whose family has produced many high-class Sidmouth players over the generations, is playing for Somerset and made his Test debut for England against Pakistan in 2018.

The club plays at Fort Field, where the militia used to train during the time of the Napoleonic wars. Over the years, spectators have seen many famous names, including Sir Jack Hobbs and Frank Woolley (both of whom scored hundreds here), Wally Hammond, Sir Viv Richards and Shane Warne. But none of them, nor indeed anyone else, has done the Sidmouth equivalent of hitting the ball over the Lord's pavilion – that is to say, swipe it clean out of the ground and into the sea, which seems so invitingly within reach. It is said that a well-struck ball once hit a lady sunbathing on the beach. Unimpressed, she

threw it into the water, which doesn't count.

Famous club performances include a Jim Laker-like 19 wicket haul in a two-innings match by the leg-spinner J. M. A. Marshall in 1948, though he was an amateur on Warwickshire's books and playing for Sidmouth as a guest while on holiday. C. T. A. Wilkinson, a home-grown player, took all 10 for 27 in 1952. He was 68 and had played for the club since 1922. It was the final game of his career, so he went out with a glorious flourish.

The ground was purchased through public subscription in 1936 and is owned by a trust which charges the club a nominal rent. The Cricket House is famous for its thatched roof, replaced every 20 years at a cost of £25,000 funded by The Friends of Fortfield. The square has an enormous eighteen pitches.

The club fields three senior sides. The Firsts and Seconds play in the Devon Cricket League and are perennial trophy-winners. To ease fixture congestion, the Thirds now play at Newton Poppleford C.C., another of the beautiful grounds in the area. There is a colts section of about 100 youngsters aged between five and 15, and a recently-formed women's section is thriving.

Club: Sidmouth C.C.

BELOW: The beautiful Regency townhouses of Fortfield Terrace overlooking Fort Field have changed little in the last hundred years.

Snettisham

Norfolk

Most villages would be satisfied with one jaw-dropping feature to leave their visitors amazed and entertained. But Snettisham is spoilt for choice. Within easy walking distance is The Wash and the RSPB reserve where thousands of wading birds can be observed taking flight. Sandringham House, the Queen's pied-à-terre in Norfolk, is only three miles away. Locally, St Mary's Church, which dominates the expansive green, is 'perhaps the most exciting decorated church in Norfolk,' according to the architectural historian Sir Nikolaus Pevsner. And Snettisham is a rare chance to see a village built from mellow locally-quarried carrstone. All that before mentioning the Snettisham Hoard of Iron Age precious metal, although you have to travel to Norwich or the British Museum to see that.

Founded in the mid-19th century, the club has played in the shadow of the soaring spire of the 14th-century church since 1947. Unsurprisingly, St Mary's was a wartime target, but remained intact, a source of great local pride and a psychological boost to succeeding generations of Snettisham batsmen, according to club chairman Tim Clarey. "If not even the mighty Luftwaffe could knock their beautiful church down, why should some opposition quickie be able to bowl their stumps over!?"

The clubhouse, also of carrstone, was built at the same time, and serves as a memorial to the local men lost in the two world wars. It must be one of the few cricket pavilions to have been blessed by the local bishop.

Snettisham runs four senior sides, including female players, and an over-40s team. There's

a thriving junior section of about 60 young players with teams at the U-15, U-13, and U-11 levels, and a budding All Stars group. The Firsts topped Division 1 of the Norfolk Cricket League in 2017 after winning every match, something never before achieved in the 50-year history of the league, gaining them promotion to the Norfolk Cricket Alliance. The Seconds were also promoted, as was the Sunday team.

Club: Snettisham C.C.

ABOVE: Snettisham seems to attract painters. Jack Russell recently stopped by the ground and professed he would like to paint the view. Already out on the boundary rope painting with oils is local artist Shawn Carey.

Southborough

Kent

Southborough C.C. has a rich cricketing history, but the club would probably agree that its prime claim to fame is playing on beautiful Southborough Common since at least 1794. The town itself was a centre of cricket ball manufacturing until 1978.

The Common today is divided more or less equally by a path. On one side, the ground falls away in the direction of Tunbridge Wells. The other half is the cricket area, not entirely without its inclines and elevations, but flat enough. The whole Common is lush and green and generously ringed by oaks with the impressive St. Peter's Church in the background. Had Constable painted cricket scenes, 'The Common, Southborough' might well have been one of his subjects.

More mundanely, the Pavilion side of the ground is bordered by the very busy A26. The club is nervous about a well-hit shot causing a traffic accident and hangs netting along the boundary just in case, as well as taking out suitable insurance.

Pre-World War I, Southborough used to be one of the top clubs in the country. A favourite son of that era was K. L. Hutchings, born there in 1880. Hutchings, described as 'possibly the most talented batsman in English cricket before the War,' played club cricket for Southborough, county cricket for Kent and in seven Test matches for England. He died in the Battle of the Somme in 1916 at the age of 33.

Almost certainly the club's greatest servant was the remarkable Lt. Col. Frank Harris who was involved as player, chairman or president from 1881 till 1957, an extraordinary 76 years. According to legend, when he was sixteen, he chased down a ball hit into some bushes. There was no formal boundary line in that area, so the batsmen were entitled to continue running. As they started out on their thirteenth run, Harris, who had used the bushes as cover, suddenly darted onto the pitch and ran one of the batsmen out.

Another Southborough story with a touch of mystery relates to Freddie Waghorn, a Second XI seamer back in the 1950s. He opened the bowling in the first game and did so well that the skipper kept him on unchanged, not just for that match but the entire season, 20 games in all. The mystery is not why he was kept on – he took 70 wickets – but why, in the last game of the season, he was taken off two overs before the end.

The club, whose Firsts and Seconds play in the Kent County Village League, uses the church clock as its official timepiece, no matter that it runs five minutes slow. Two trees in front of the church have been noticeably trimmed so that the clock face is visible from the field. Elsewhere, two more trees lie inside the boundary. The more distant one earns six if hit on the full. The nearer tree is worth four whether hit on the full or not. A fielder in that area should take care he does not brush even one leaf throwing the ball back, otherwise that will cost four as well. At the end of the day's play, with the sun beginning to sink behind the church and the far side of the ground in shadow, much pleasure can be had from watching the closing overs seated on a bench beside the pavilion (with your back to the A26).

Club: Southborough C.C.

Southill Park

Bedfordshire

Southill Park C.C., founded in 1884, plays on the beautiful Whitbread Estate near Biggleswade in Bedfordshire. It's been the home of the Whitbread brewing family for hundreds of years and a member of the family is always club president. "We are privileged to play here," says chairman Martin Darlow, "it's such a beautiful ground," adding that the club is in as good a place as it has ever been.

On the field, the Saturday first team plays in the Cambridgeshire and Huntingdonshire Premier League Division 2. Two more promotions will see it in the top division. The club runs seven adult teams, including Sunday and midweek sides, drawing on a nucleus of 60 players. "There's a pretty good mix," says Darlow. "The older players have been strengthened by younger players who only a couple of summers ago were playing very successfully at youth level." Just beginning to climb the cricketing ladder are about 40 juniors, boys and girls, who turn up for training once a week and enjoy the BBQ prepared for them and their parents.

In May 2016 Martin was invited to join the ECB as the recreational game representative. So every few weeks he's off to Lord's to meet Chairman Colin Graves and other luminaries such as Andrew Strauss, Claire Connor and Steve Elworth, dealing with the cricketing issues of the day. "I've got a free 'Access All Area' pass to every ground in the country," says Darlow, a former policeman, who still plays occasionally, "but I always pay".

Recent improvements include state-of-the-art outdoor nets, better sightscreens, a little TLC for the outstandingly lovely thatched scorebox, and upgraded kitchens and showers for the pavilion. A more modern roller is on the wish list. The large square with sixteen strips is well managed by Head Groundsman John Wissen, helped by Graeme Lamb, his assistant, and a number of team members.

Club: Southill Park CC

OPPOSITE: Like Shobrooke Park in Devon the ground is ringed by magnificent cedars; the one to the right is within the playing area.

BELOW: The beautiful thatched pavilion and scoreboard.

Spout House

North Yorkshire

Even if you knew there was a cricket ground in the vicinity, Spout House would be easy to miss. Driving north from Helmsley, don't be distracted by the grandeur of the ruins of Rievaulx Abbey, but keep on the B1275. The North York Moors, dotted with sheep, begin to climb steeply.

After about ten miles of anxiously wondering if you haven't somehow missed it, a pub looms up on the right, the Sun Inn. Pubs in the middle of nowhere are not uncommon in Yorkshire, but with no obvious local village, you do wonder what its catchment area is.

Until only a few years ago, the Sun was run by the Ainsley family, principally grandfather William and grandson William George. Next to the pub a field runs down (gradient: one in seven) to a stone wall which borders the road. The field is part of a working farm run by the next generation of the Ainsley family.

Halfway down, the slope levels out for a few yards and is almost flat. The shaggy grass becomes miraculously short and even. You have stumbled across the Spout House square with three pitches, invisible from the road. The flatness is not a topographical oddity. In the corner of the field next to a rickety wooden shed, which turns out to be the pavilion, is a magnificent Victorian sandstone roller, possibly the only working model of its kind in existence. Before matches, teams of six or seven manhandle it up and down the pitch to achieve an impressive flatness. Ground rules include the square leg umpire standing on the off side when the bowling is from the pub end in order to see the popping crease. Calling 'lost ball' when the ball disappears in the grass will certainly save a few runs.

If farming was the Ainsleys' living, running Spout House cricket team, founded in the mid-19th century, was their passion. Grandfather and grandson ran the club for an amazing, unbroken joint span of 138 years which came to an end in 2012 when William George died. Their memorial stones, side by side, are set into the north wall of the field. The team carries on, thanks to a small band of dedicated cricket lovers. It competes in the Feversham League which was reduced to only three teams, where it once had a dozen or so. Thankfully it has found a fourth and should continue. It is hard to imagine cricket dying out in Yorkshire of all places.

Enough enthusiasm remains for Spout House to play a Friday evening away game. Farndale is in the middle of the Moors, not too far away as the crow flies, but a fair drive as there is no direct link road. As at Spout, the cricket field can contain a hundred sheep which are ushered down the slope to the fence before a game. After matches the teams adjourn to the nearby Feversham Arms, where Farndale's cricket trophies are prominently displayed. Let us hope they will continue to do so for many more seasons.

Club: Spout House C.C.

ABOVE RIGHT: Nobody could accuse Spout House of manicuring their pitch. First and foremost, it's a sheep field.

RIGHT: The ancient roller only gets the occasional trundle these days.

BELOW: Tea taken all together on one long table – that's proper Yorkshire.

Stanton

Gloucestershire

Built of locally-quarried honey-coloured limestone and set against the backdrop of Bredon Hill and the distant Malverns, the small village of Stanton is one of the prettiest in the Cotswolds. Dating back to the 16th century, it was bought by the engineer and architect Sir Philip Stott in 1906. Stott immediately set about major restoration work, renovating the local cottages, completing a reservoir and building a swimming pool for local children. As every English village needs a team to rally round, he also built a cricket field on a pasture adjacent to his home, Stanton Court, a striking Jacobean manor house once the property of Queen Katherine Parr.

St. Philips North C.C. are relatively recent arrivals, succeeding various village sides which had played here over the years. The club had been happily settled at Dowty Arle Court in Cheltenham, a lovely park once painted by former England wicket-keeper Jack Russell. But around the turn of the millennium, the owners developed the land for housing, leaving a much-reduced playing area unsuitable for adult cricket.

Forced to move on, the club was in limbo while it looked for a new ground – without luck until Stanton Court became available in 2007. "It was well worth waiting for," says treasurer Craig Sprigmore. "We get on very well with our landlords and who wouldn't love playing here? We've no trouble recruiting players, mainly from the Cheltenham area, because they want to play in such wonderful surroundings."

The Firsts play in Division 7 of the Gloucestershire County League, having won every game in 2017 to earn promotion. St. Philips North also runs a Second XI, a midweek T20 side and a team in the Indoor Sixes league in the off-season. The club cares for the playing area itself, a team effort under the direction of groundsman Martin Enstone. The old 4-ton diesel roller bought second hand is still well used.

Teas are a high spot of each home game with the traditional sandwiches and cakes catered for by a combination of the wife of the Second XI captain and the club members on a rota basis. With no bar in the attractive but compact pavilion, post-match refreshments are enjoyed in the local pub, The Mount. The club takes pride in its hospitality and welcomes visitors as day members, an offer taken up by many hikers along the Cotswold Way.

As Craig Sprigmore says, "Competitive cricket – friendly and beautiful surroundings – who could ask for anything more?"

Club: St. Philips North C.C.

BOTTOM: Stanton village is filled with an array of beautiful Cotswold stone cottages.

Stanway

Gloucestershire

Stanton and Stanway, are cheek-by-jowl in this book and only a couple of miles apart in Gloucestershire. The principal landmark of the small tranquil village of Stanway in Gloucestershire is undoubtedly Stanway House, and the imposing Stanway Gate, a Jacobean gem owned and occupied by the Earls of Wemyss and March and their ancestors since 1533. But the cricket club, just off the Cotswold Way on the road out of the village, is equally beautiful in its own way. Set in idyllic countryside against the backdrop of hills, the ground has some very interesting features and a famous association with the writer J. M. Barrie, author of *Peter Pan*.

Cricket has been played at Stanway since 1877 when, according to a record in Stanway House, the ground could be hired for 5 shillings. If that sounds good value, the £10 it pays the current Earl today is almost certainly less after allowing for inflation. The Earl is the club's president and takes a very close and practical interest in the club's affairs. For its part, the club honours his preference that it plays a home match on the day of the Stanway Fete in July, held in the grounds of Stanway House.

J. M. Barrie's association with Stanway began in 1921 when he was a guest at the House. He visited it frequently until his death in 1937, often inviting cricket-loving guests, including the entire Australian touring party of 1921, who certainly would have tried out a few shots at the nearby park.

Barrie had form as a cricket fanatic. He founded his own team, the Allahakbarries, which ran for about 20 years up to the beginning of World War I and filled it with cricket-besotted writers such as H. G. Wells, whose father was a professional cricketer; P. G. Wodehouse, who named his comic creation Jeeves after a promising young Warwickshire cricketer who did not survive World War I, and Sir Arthur Conan Doyle, who played first-class cricket and once bowled out W. G. Grace.

In 1925, Barrie initiated and paid for the construction of a new pavilion to celebrate taking a hat-trick, or so it is said. Built by a local Winchcombe builder, it rests on 25 very unusual mushroom-shaped saddle stones, normally used under granaries to keep them clear of vermin. The timber frame, clad with larch poles and capped with a thatched roof, gives it a pleasant, rustic ambience. The space beneath the Grade II-listed pavilion is a useful storage area.

The ground in a meadow off the main road is a large playing area of 6 acres. It takes three hours for mowers to achieve an immaculate smoothness, although ancient ridges, vestiges of the old strip system of agriculture, create undulations which have been known to disconcert visiting fieldsmen. The antique (1950) roller has just been retired and replaced by a more modern (1975) cricket roller.

Many famous names have visited the ground. Returning from Australia in 1933, the then Earl of Wemys found himself on the same liner as the infamous bodyline England cricket team and arranged a match at Stanway in support of local hospitals. The complete Gloucestershire county side, including Wally Hammond and Tom Goddard, played The Earl's guest XI, which featured Herbert Sutcliffe, the Nawab of Pataudi, Maurice Leyland, R. E. S. Wyatt and Gubby Allen – the England side in all but name.

The club runs just the one side in the Cotswold Hills League and says it is becoming harder to raise a team, although the numbers of promising youngsters are growing. When Stanway don't need the ground, it is often used for hire games, sometimes supplemented by beer brewed on the estate, which can be delivered by wheelbarrow.

Club: Stanway C.C.

TOP: J. M. Barrie promised to buy the club a pavilion if he took a hat-trick in a match. The story goes that this feat of cricketing prowess owed more to the complicity of the opposition than James Matthew's ability with the ball.

RIGHT: The old medieval strip system is very much in evidence away from the square.

Stoneleigh Abbey

Warwickshire, England

Cricket has been played in this superb setting since 1839 when Sir Chandos Leigh laid out a ground for his son William to play on during his hols from Harrow School. Stoneleigh Abbey was once a monastery dating back to the 12th century. It came into the possession of the Leigh family in the 16th century after the Dissolution of the Monasteries when it was converted into a large country house.

It was William's younger brother Edward who went on to achieve cricketing prominence in Varsity matches. He played in three winning Oxford University teams from 1852-4, though he scored a total of only eight runs in all the matches and may well have owed his place to his specialist fielding at long-stop. The first significant match on the ground took place in 1849 when the club played Rugby School.

Edward's last game was in 1872 aged 40 when 'Fourteen Gentlemen of Warwickshire' played a two-day game against the well-known wanderers I Zingari. His playing days over, he continued to involve himself in cricket and became President of the MCC in 1887.

The Abbey is now converted to flats and owned by a trust. The *noblesse oblige* connection has

also disappeared, which, more than one hundred years ago, rewarded one of the Stoneleigh batsman with a sixpence from Lord Leigh for hitting a six though one of the main floor windows. However cricket continues to thrive and Stoneleigh C.C. plays in the Cotswold Hills League against teams with evocative names like Long Itchington. Lord Leigh also owned an estate in Adlestrop, the village in Gloucestershire made

famous by Edward Thomas's poem, and there is an annual fixture between the two villages for the Lord Leigh Cup.

The ground is unchanging in its charm and won the 2003 *Wisden Cricketer* prize for the most beautiful ground in England. Perhaps its essence was best caught all those years ago in 1872 by John Loraine Baldwin writing as the game

against I Zingari drew to its close: 'When all was finished there seemed a lingering desire on both sides not to leave the ground, as they gazed at the old Abbey calm and beautiful in its grandeur…'

Club: Stoneleigh C.C.

Tilford Green

Surrey

According to a minute book in Farnham Museum, Tilford C.C. was formed in 1886. However the club is quite sure that cricket was played on the lovely green well before that. The argument goes that the Hambledon legend 'Silver Billy' Beldham – once rated as the best batsman in the world – moved to Tilford in 1822 and lived there until his death at the age of 96 in 1862. Understandably, no-one believes he would have lived in a cricket-free zone. And the green is such a tempting space for a game…

'Silver Billy' was landlord of the The Barley Mow, a local institution which has long been the cricket team's unofficial clubhouse. His ghost is said to still haunt the 18th-century alehouse. Another building on the opposite boundary really *is* an institution. The Tilford Institute was designed by the great Victorian architect, Sir Edwin Lutyens in 1894 as a focus for sport, and is the cricket club's official address as well as its pavilion

Tilford has played in the I'Anson League – reputedly the oldest continuously-operating village cricket league in the country – since 1904. The club got up to speed very swiftly, winning a hat-trick of league titles from 1908-1910. As was the custom, the cup became their property. But without a trophy to play for, no-one was sure if there would be a competition the following season. Mr. I'Anson came to the rescue and

LEFT: Unlike many cricket grounds, Tilford has a rectangle not a square, with a few pitches to the right of the wicket where the wicket-keeper and slips are standing.

provided a replacement, though clubs winning three successive league titles are no longer entitled to retain the trophy.

Tilford has produced many fine cricketers over the years, but one in particular stands out – William James Eddey, a slow to medium-paced bowler. According to Graham Collyer's centenary history, no-one knows how many wickets he took in his 40-year career, 'but it was probably nearer 20,000 than 10,000'. He almost always took 100 wickets a season and his haul in 1949 was a barely believable 268 wickets at an average of 5.25.

Collyer also tells of the unusual occasion in 1936 when a Tilford game was broadcast live on BBC, sharing the stage with a Test match between England and India. When the quacking of the local ducks caused a problem, the BBC had to reduce their volume. The commentator, Lt. Cdr Woodroffe, told a local reporter: "This is cricket as it should be played. The game started like this on the village green…I would rather be here than at the Test match in Manchester.'

Club: Tilford C.C.

TOP: The Edwin Lutyens-designed Tilford Institute is the club's pavilion.

Triangle

Yorkshire

It sounds like a work of fiction from the late Peter Tinniswood, or worthy of a song by Jake Thackray, but Triangle C.C. play their cricket at Grassy Bottom in the Halifax Cricket League. The Grassy Bottom ground is one of a fine quartet of captivating grounds from the league that make it into this book and through the season the First XI will play at Booth, Copley and Mytholmroyd.

Another seeming Tinniswood-ism is the story that when the team played away at local villages, they would take a carrier pigeon with them. After the game was finished they would strap the result to the bird's leg and send it back to the pigeon loft behind the Triangle pub where their local supporters would be drinking. Thus villagers knew the score before the team returned home.

The club started life in 1862 as the Triangle Reading Room and Cricket Club and has doubled as a sports club and working man's club through its lifetime. In 1927 local mill owner Colonel Tom Morris gifted the ground on Stansfield Mill Lane to the club and so the only great peril is the river Ryburn which runs close to the boundary's edge. In fact one of the great charms of the club is said to be listening to the sound of rushing water on a sunny day while sitting on one of the many wooden benches while watching a game of cricket.

It is located midway between Sowerby Bridge and Ripponden, and it is Sowerby St. Peters who are the big local rivals. The facilities at the club have been upgraded over the years with the scoreboard being removed from the top of the two-story pavilion in 1982 and taken to the far end of the ground to bookend proceedings.

There is still strong support from players in an area stacked with cricket teams. Triangle put out a First and Second XI along with a Sunday XI and since 1903 have won the Parish Cup 12 times. Since 1896 they have been Division 1 Champions 18 times, and though Christian Silkstone is their current leading batsman, it has to be noted that in 2006 Lachlan Sculley scored 1116 runs averaging 93 but still didn't win the League batting prize.

Club: Triangle C.C.

Ullenwood

Gloucestershire

Ullenwood cricket ground, home of Ullenwood Bharat C.C., is hidden away near one of the busiest junctions between Gloucester, Cheltenham and Cirencester, known to all as the Air Balloon roundabout. Aim for Crickley Hill Country Park and you will find the playing area in a large undulating meadow at the foot of the access road. Well sheltered as it is by horse chestnuts and other trees, they cannot quite deaden the sound of the traffic grumbling by.

Ullenwood Bharat is a merger of two clubs, Ullenwood C.C. and Bharat C.C. Ullenwood has suffered more than its fair share of anxieties and bad luck in recent years, starting on New Year's Eve 2006, when vandals burnt down the pavilion. Unfortunately, the insurance didn't fully cover the cost of a rebuild. Generous donations from the club's supporters provided the cash to buy the raw materials for a new pavilion, which the members erected themselves over a period of time. Meanwhile, without decent facilities, players left the club and one season the club had to cancel all its Sunday fixtures because it couldn't raise a team. Finally, the club appealed to Gloucestershire County Council to sell them the ground for £25,000, the cost to be financed by Sport England. This arrangement appeared to be going through until the unexpected happened. "Two fatal road accidents occurred nearby," explains Tony Webb, club secretary for the last 25 years, "and the Council put the sale on hold until a new road system was sorted out."

However, Tony Webb is nothing if not resilient. Hearing that a local club, Bharat C.C., was searching for another ground, a merger seemed the obvious answer. "Ullenwood had the ground and Bharat had the numbers," Tony says.

The merger took place in 2012 and five years later, it is clear it has worked out very well. The club has almost 60 members and runs teams on Saturdays, Sundays and in midweek. The Firsts compete very successfully in the Gloucestershire County Cricket League and have been promoted in each of the last four seasons. Ullenwood Bharat is especially proud of its exceptionally diverse ethnic mix of Indian, Pakistani, West Indian, South African, English, Afghanistani and Scottish players. Another talking point is the oak tree just inside the boundary. Many years ago, someone argued that if a shot hit the tree, it wasn't worth four or six as the ball hadn't crossed the boundary. In a typical committee compromise, it was decided that the shot was worth three, signalled by drawing a tree shape in the air.

The future may well be as interesting as the recent past. With the club growing and the council still considering its traffic layout plans, Tony Webb has somehow positioned the club to become the owners of a cricket ground on the site of an old ICI factory in nearby Brockworth. In the meantime, the club cheerfully puts up with the mole and rabbit droppings and an overflowing pond…

Club: Ullenwood Bharat C.C.

Uplyme

Dorset

There's nothing historians like better than a good row about dates, and while some sources believe Uplyme Cricket Club was founded in 1886, others believe it was 1877. There is no dispute that they have been playing cricket on the Glebe Field near the Talbot Arms in Uplyme since the end of the 19th century (the playing area was subsequently renamed as King George V Playing Field). The Lyme Regis Cricket Club dates to 1862 and the two clubs joined forces in 1935 to play on Uplyme's pitch further inland, well away from all the fossil hunters and those recreating scenes from Thomas Hardy novels on Lyme Regis's famous Cobb.

Despite residing in Dorset, the club looks westward for its cricket. It enters two Saturday teams in the Devon Cricket League and also fields a friendly side in Sunday and midweek competitions.

There is a classic photo taken in front of the old pavilion of a 1975 testimonial match for Somerset and England bowler Tom Cartwright, when a Somerset XI took on Uplyme and Lyme Regis. Amongst various famous cricketing faces in the joint photo are Tom Cartwright and Brian Close at the end of their careers, and a fresh-faced Ian Botham and Vic Marks.

That classic older pavilion, square of the wicket, has now been usurped by a more modern facility just behind the village hall and the old wooden

structure has been claimed by the Lyme Valley Croquet Club – which plays two different forms of croquet.

With active U-11, U-13 and U-15 teams the club is thriving and adding improvements; last year the club put on a one-day T20 competition to raise money for some new covers. Local teams Seaton, Kilmington and Axminster competed with Uplyme and Lyme Regis for the one-day trophy, a format that may well be repeated in the future.

Club: Uplyme and Lyme Regis C.C.

BELOW RIGHT: The croquet club have taken possession of the old cricket pavilion, while the more recent pavilion is much closer to the village hall.

Warborough Green

Oxfordshire

It must be the ultimate compliment – a setting so beautiful that teams queue up to play there. Take a look at Warborough and Shillingford's fixture list and you won't find a single away game. The club plays only home friendlies, though they are competitive enough. Visitors are not local village sides but teams with esoteric names like the Proper Job XI, Captain Scott Invitation XI and The Luddites. No Sundays off for the tea ladies, then, a chore usually delegated to the WAG/mother of that week's team manager. The tempting refreshments are set out on wooden picnic tables under the oaks, perfect surroundings of the most traditional English type.

Cricket on the Green is first mentioned in the diary of Maria Tubb, 20, on May 19th, 1831, when the home side beat (or were beaten by) neighbouring village Milton – the entry in papers held by the Bodleian Library is ambiguous.

The expansive Green can also accommodate a separate rugby or football pitch and is bordered on three sides by sycamores, limes, horse chestnut trees and oaks. Beyond the perimeter road lies 13th-century St. Laurence's Church. Walk to the edge of the ground on the fourth side and nothing stands between you and the Chilterns in the distance. If the scene looks vaguely familiar, think of one of those TV drama series set in idyllic village surroundings where the murder rate is astronomically above the national average. Warborough village and its pub, The Six Bells, have been used as a location for *Midsomer Murders*, as well as episodes of *Jeeves and Wooster*.

The club has particularly strong and amiable links with Somerset CCC dating back to 1981. The county side has visited the club on many occasions for benefit games, bringing stars like Sir Ian Botham, Sir Viv Richards and Steve Waugh. Another immortal, Joel Garner, hit nine sixes in an innings including a tremendous effort over the lime trees at the north end of the ground.

Warborough & Shillingford's current cricket is very vibrant and buzzes with the performance of pace bowler Tim Chamberlain. In 2017, he took all 10 wickets against Captain Scott's XI. The club has an excellent record in youth cricket over the years. Many have played representative cricket in their age groups. It currently runs teams for five different age groups from the U-7s to the U-15s, each team with its own manager. Under the direction of Chris Ward, the colts make much use – more than the seniors, in fact – of two new state-of-the-art nets and of the bowling machine, purchased through the money-raising efforts of the club chairman, Jonnie Bradshaw, so their success is likely to continue.

Club: Warborough and Shillingford C.C.

TOP: The pavilion is owned by the Parish Council. On the front is a plaque in memory of Rev. Herbert White, thanks to whom the Green wasn't enclosed in 1853, or, as the plaque colourfully puts it, "…who saved the green from Goths and Utilitarians."

RIGHT: The club doesn't need a bar because the Six Bells is only a few yards away. While you're there, treat yourself to a pint of Golden Duck in a good cause –10% of the proceeds are pumped back into club funds.

Warkworth Castle

Northumberland

Warkworth Castle is a grand, extensive ruin in Northumberland — on a good day within sight of the River Coquet estuary. There was a time in the Middle Ages when it was the fortress home of the Earls of Northumberland. Shakespeare set several scenes of *Henry IV Parts I and II* in the castle, one of them involving the hot-blooded Harry Hotspur, depicted like Freddie Trueman bowling off a long run.

These days, the Grade I-listed castle is a popular tourist destination. Unlike many sides linked to a historic building, Warkworth didn't start off as an estates team, but has always been a village side, collecting its players from Warkworth and neighbouring communities. "It's a strong family club," says secretary Alastair Gibson. "Families like the Pringles and the Dargues have played for Warkworth for generations."

Despite its relatively small catchment area, the club has a record to be proud of, winning the Northumberland League Premier Division seven times and the Thomas Wilson Cup, a knockout competition, on nine occasions, most recently in 2011. It has hosted various All-Star teams and celebrated its centenary in 1975 with a game between a Rohan Kanhai XI and a Deryck Murray XI. Warkworth, which runs three teams, is proud of its performance in the National Village Knockout competition, reaching the quarter-finals on one occasion and being knocked out on another by a Lancashire village side containing the 17-year-old Mike Atherton.

Until 1963, the pavilion was an old railway carriage in the corner of the field dating back to the 1920s or earlier. Gibson is praying nothing untoward will happen to the current pavilion. "If it gets burnt down," he says, "we might not be able to get planning permission to rebuild it." No sightscreen is allowed at the castle end of the ground and the one in front of the houses at the other end is very discreet.

Much of the club's income comes from bar takings and fund-raising events, such as the annual Golf Day and September Walkfest. It is trying to raise £11,000 for a new outfield mower to make the jobs of groundsmen Jack Dargue, Keith Douglas and Ken Middlemass a little easier.

Club: Warkworth Castle C.C.

White Coppice

Lancashire

The setting for White Coppice C.C. at the foot of the West Pennine Moors is stunning with heather-clad slopes, lush trees and grazing sheep as a backdrop. A good-sized brook runs down one side of the ground and is a tempting target for batters. They're economical folk in these parts and all balls are fished out, not replaced. The white cottages beyond the boundary used to double up as a sightscreen, although the club has now purchased the real thing. Even so, the ground's 8-foot drop means a maximum can still hit the cottages, despite the protective netting. There's plenty of wet weather around, according to Mark Fishwick, a club elder and former wicket-keeper, "but fortunately the ground dries quickly. The real problem is the clouds of midges which can sometimes stop play!"

A progressive local mill owner, Ephraim Eccles, founded the club in 1875. How interested he was in cricket is not known. Possibly the exercise was a good way of keeping his mill workers fit. He was a strong supporter of the Temperance movement and to this day there is no alcohol available in White Coppice or nearby Angelzarke.

The club is not without recent successes, but, according to Mark Fishwick, White Coppice's best days go back 30 years or more. After recent reorganisation, the club now runs one senior side mainly drawn from the Chorley area and plays in Divison 2 of the Palace Shield Competition. Financially, the club owes much to Geoff Haydock, a member for over 50 years, 30 of them as sponsorship secretary. His initiatives include organising a very successful annual sportsmen's dinner, so that the balance sheet is in good shape. The current pavilion is the club's third and has recently been refurbished with the help of generous local donations and grants. Thanks to Mr. Eccles, there is no bar income, but excellent teas are provided by the Coppice Café, which is also open to the public in summer months.

The ground has appeared many times on calendars and in magazines and also featured in the 1994 BBC television drama *The Sloggers*. Through the magic of television, a clock tower was added to the pavilion and the cottages opposite were turned into a pub, *The Fallen Wicket*. But the guest appearance of Geoff Boycott was real enough and is well-remembered.

Club: White Coppice C.C.

Wingfield

Wiltshire

It's been said in the past that cricket has a drinking culture. Well, this place isn't going to help. Not only is The Poplars Inn, in Wingfield, a beautiful pub to sit outside with one of the finest pints of ale that England has to offer – Wadworth's 6X – it also has its own cricket pitch.

Judging from the on-field banter of an evening T20 game against Frome Incidentals in 2017, the Poplars cricket team don't take their cricket too seriously. At one point in the match the Frome scorer shouts out for the name of the new bowler and square-leg helpfully suggests, "just put 'fatty waddling in, right arm over'". Sledging is supposed to be against the opposition, not your own side.

The pub cricket team has been running for over 50 years now, and celebrated its half-century in 2017 with what the *Wiltshire Times* described as 'a light-hearted game that ended in a draw, with both teams getting 164 runs off 25 overs'.

"It was just the perfect way to celebrate 50 years of cricket at the club. When you think of all the cricket teams that have folded over the years, it is remarkable that a social club, that does not enter into leagues or competitions and just plays for the love of the game, is still going strong," says Clive Warren, captain of the Poplars' side.

The pitch is a compact one, and the eponymous poplars line the boundary to the main road, Shop Lane. Such is the proximity of the boundary on that side of the square that any blow that clears the ropes is deemed six-and-out.

Despite the fantastic venue, there are not many opportunities to view a game in progress, with just 13 home games in 2018. Highlights of the fixture list are the Presidents/Village match at the end of August, and a visit from Canterbury (Australia) C.C. at the end of July, for which a few extra barrels of 6X may well be ordered in.

Club: Poplars C.C.

Winnington Park

Northwich, Cheshire

Northwich isn't everybody's idea of a traditional English village, but Winnington Park's inclusion is on the basis that village teams do play cricket at their ground. Northwich C.C. is the town's main cricket club, and few local grounds have such a dramatic industrial backdrop for their games. If the redundant gas holder (now listed) at the Kennington Oval has become a much-admired element of the landscape, then the former ICI chemical works is a prodigious beauty.

School geography lessons taught us that the Romans mined salt in north Cheshire. The extraction of salt gave rise to soda-ash factories and spawned the Brunner Mond/ICI chemical businesses at various sites including Winnington. Indeed, the first practical method for producing polythene was discovered by Brunner Mond at the Winnington works in 1933.

Winnington Park Recreation Club was originally the company's sports ground, hosting a variety of sports on impeccably manicured surfaces. The grand, half-timbered pavilion is reminiscent of the Bournville cricket pavilion in Birmingham built by the Cadbury empire.

Cricket has been played at Winnington Park since the 1880s. Only friendly fixtures were played until the Recreation Club joined the Manchester and District Cricket Association in 1921. Cricket Secretary at the time A. H. S. Guthrie remarked in his annual notes that 1929 saw the Club at the centre of an occurrence worthy of inclusion in *Wisden*. 'A tie is a rare result in cricket but against Bollington, in 1929, Winnington Park forced a tie not only in the first XI fixture at home, but also in the second eleven match played on the same day at Bollington.'

In 1975 the club won the mid-Cheshire knockout cup, the same year they left the Manchester Association to become founder members of the Cheshire County Cricket League. In the early 1990s the Recreation Club was sold to its members, allowing profits to be used to improve the various sports clubs facilities. Today Winnington Park Cricket Club have a First and Second XI and run three junior teams in the Cheshire County Cricket League, and the North Cheshire Junior Cricket Association and are proud of the fact they are the only Cheshire club to have won the National U-15s Championship, having lifted the trophy in 1989.

Club: Winnington Park C.C.

LEFT: The industrial site is now owned by Tata Chemicals and many of the redundant industrial buildings are not long for this world.

Author's Notes

Virtually all the stories and background information about the 90-plus grounds in this book came first-hand from the clubs themselves. As written histories were few and far between, Plan A was to try and reach the chairman or secretary. But this was not as simple as it sounded. More often than not, the only contact number given was the clubhouse. Most of my research was done during the winter and I quickly realised that the phone was often ringing in an empty, shuttered pavilion.

Forced to think laterally, I found that the parish council website could be a good source. The community-minded individual who was chairman of the village cricket club was sometimes a parish councillor with a phone number. If that drew a blank, I tried to reach the Clerk to the Parish Council. Even if he or she couldn't help me directly, I was often given a number to phone. That is why I occasionally found myself talking to the local vicar who'd last played for the team a couple of decades earlier. He was fairly sure he knew how to reach the ex-secretary, who turned out to have left the district a few years ago. And so on. Other sources in extremis were the local cricket league or even a neighbouring club. Explaining that I was trying to reach their deadly rivals for an article in a high-quality illustrated book could have provoked an unhelpful response, except that rivalry was always left on the cricket field.

As well as telephone contact, I enjoyed visiting nearly a quarter of the grounds, among them Spout House, Raby Castle, Sheepscombe and Knole Park. They and all the other venues were as stunningly idiosyncratic as you'd expect. But turning up on match days wasn't such a bright idea, as the people I had come to see were usually otherwise engaged in batting, fielding or scoring. Without exception, the atmosphere was relaxed and friendly, the cricket keen and competitive, and the teas excellent. As I lounged in a deckchair at the edge of the boundary, it struck me that, while some of the batting may have been village, much of the banter was Test standard, though with a softer edge.

For those clubs I didn't get to visit, I crafted a questionnaire. But I quickly found it was a blunt tool and drew only monosyllabic factual answers. As soon as I resorted to personal contact, the conversation opened up and drew some revealing anecdotes. Ebernoe is very proud of its unique annual Horn Fair Day match, with a pair of ram's horns awarded to the highest-scoring batsman. At Arthington the dazzling sun in the batsmen's eyes means bowling takes place from one end only at certain times. At Sheepscombe and Bilsington the slope of the ground means a fielder on the boundary is totally unsighted and has to be alerted by his teammates that the ball is heading their way. At Linkenholt, the remarkable Elsie Smith has been club secretary (plus other roles) since 1946. The fallow deer at Knole Park have right of way, even on the cricket field; and Patterdale plays on 'the prettiest field in England', according to no less an authority than William Wordsworth.

The size of the clubs ranged enormously. Some ran one Saturday XI, playing only friendlies. Others were like mini-corporations with six senior teams in a highly organised regional league and many junior sides. Almost everyone I spoke to held more than one position, often a combination of chairman, secretary and groundsman. The continued existence of village cricket is very much in their hands, but they are not getting any younger. More than once I was told that successors were thin on the ground. There was also some concern about the lack of younger players, although many clubs were hugely involved with youth cricket for both boys and girls. A good number of clubs pay peppercorn or non-commercial rents and acknowledge their debt to their landlords, whether a generous private individual, the local Estate or the council. Organisations like the ECB and Sport England often provided significant funding, which was much appreciated.

Brian Levison 2018
(by Baldon Green pavilion)

Index

Index

Photo

Alamy: 13, 18, 28, 29, 40, 48, 49, 50, 51, 53, 54, 55, 58, 59, 62, 73, 74, 75, 80, 81, 82, 83, 86, 87, 88, 89, 132, 138, 139, 148, 152, 154, 155, 162, 163, 182, 183.

Biggleswade Chronicle: 106.

DalesEyeView: 44.

Alan Duncan Photography: 4, 120, 122, 165.

Firle Cricket Club: 85.

Getty Images: 36, 45, 126.

Honley Cricket Club: 101.

Frank Hopkinson for Pavilion Books: 6, 7, 9, 10, 11, 14, 15, 16, 17, 33, 34, 35, 38, 39, 46, 47, 64, 66, 67, 84, 98, 99, 106, 107, 108, 109, 110, 111, 118, 119, 124, 125, 128, 129, 134, 135, 145, 146, 147, 158, 159, 178, 179, 184, 185, 187, 188, 189, 194, 195, 196, 197, 198, 199, 202, 204, 205, 210, 211, 212, 213, 218, 219, 222.

Linkenholt Cricket Club: 127

David Major: 7, 8. 20, 21, 22, 23, 25, 26, 30, 56, 57, 60, 61, 68, 69, 70, 71, 76, 78, 79, 90, 91, 92, 93, 94, 95, 96, 97, 100, 112, 113, 114, 115, 116, 117, 130, 131 140, 141, 142, 143, 150, 151, 156, 157, 160, 161, 168, 169, 170, 171, 172, 173, 174, 175, 206, 207, 208, 209, 214, 215, 216, 217, 220, 221.

Gordon McKinnie: 77.

Jill Mead: 24, 25, 26, 27, 52, 102, 103, 104, 105, 180, 181, 190, 192, 193, 222.

John Needham: 136, 137.

Liz O'Sullivan: 166.

PinPoint Media: 176, 177.

Mark A. Roberts: 42.

William Steyn: 64.

Stourbridge News: 94.

Kerry Young: 200.

Entries for Benenden, Coldharbour, Ickwell, Knightshayes Court, Longparish, Oxted, Ramsbottom, Shobrooke Park, Triangle, Uplyme and Winnington Park written by Salamander Books editorial.